SHANE LESLIE'S

GHOST
BOOK

SHANE LESLIE'S
GHOST
BOOK

by

Shane Leslie

'Bona Tempora Volvant'

Arcadia
MMXVII

Printed in the United States of America

ISBN 978-1-944339-07-4

Ghost Book
Copyright © 2017 by Tumblar House

Visit our website at www.tumblarhouse.com

Table of Contents

FOREWORD

Charles A. Coulombe

THAT the dead can return to the living is an article of Catholic Faith—indeed, *the* article of Catholic Faith if we are speaking of the Resurrection of Jesus Christ, without which, as St. Paul tells us, our Faith is vain. But Our Lord was most definitely *not* a ghost or spirit, as He made most clear Himself. What of apparitions, then? Since Our Lady's death and bodily Assumption into Heaven, she has appeared repeatedly to the Faithful; so too have scores of the Saints. But these heavenly visitations are hardly what most of us mean by that chilling word: *ghost*. The book you are reading is a professedly Catholic attempt to deal with that particular class of revenants; in my humble opinion, it is the best such attempt thus far.

Shane Leslie's Ghost Book first appeared in 1956, at a time when mention of the author, Sir Shane Leslie (1885-1971), in the title, was enough to confer on the book a certain authority. Sir Shane was a scion of a family of the Anglo-Irish ascendancy, settled at Castle Leslie in County Monaghan since time out of mind (and happily still so settled). He was Winston Churchill's First Cousin, their mothers having been sisters. But in 1908, this pillar of the Protestant establishment became a Catholic—in the same year as his friend G.K. Chesterton. Indeed, Sir Shane made his name as a British/Irish Catholic convert writer in that golden era between the wars, so filled with so many such scribes—most if not of all of whom he knew. Sir Shane's

1

wandering pen took him into many areas; by the time he sat down to write of ghosts from a Catholic perspective, he had won a well-deserved reputation for both orthodoxy and talent.

It is clear from a reading of this book that he was partly inspired to write by *Lord Halifax's Ghost Book*, which had come out twenty years earlier. Sir Shane had known the author of that book, Charles Wood, 2nd Viscount Halifax (1839 – 1934), quite well. Lord Halifax was quite wealthy, a leading Papalist Anglo-Catholic (he conducted the Malines Conversations with Belgium's Cardinal Mercier in hopes of reuniting the Church of England with Rome, and would no doubt be very happy with to-day's Anglican Ordinariates), and a splendid host. Much given to house parties, it was in that latter capacity that he invited guests to jot down tales of haunting they believed to be true in a note-book. Together with his own experiences, this was the core of the *Ghost Book* published in his name after his death by his son Edward—successively Viceroy of India, Foreign Minister, wartime ambassador to Washington, and 1st Earl of Halifax, who shared his father's religious and political views. Echoes of the work of the Lords Halifax will be found in this book—Sir Shane knew at least as well as they did how to retell a good ghost story!

But Sir Shane had a bigger end in sight than mere passing on a few pleasant chills. His stories are all Catholic themed—and before recounting them he delves into both what Catholic theology has to say about ghosts and what the Church has declared permissible for Catholics in terms of research in the area. He reminds us that while Catholics are forbidden to participate in séances and the like (and we may include the use of Ouija boards in that prohibition), in his day at any rate Catholics were granted permission to join in the work of such bodies as the Society for Psychical Research and the Ghost Club under careful ecclesiastical supervision.

This need not surprise us. In the aftermath of World War I with its mountains of dead soldiers, sailors, Spiritualism and Theosophy became very popular in Britain. It was a time when even such as Sir Arthur Conan Doyle, apostate Catholic turned rationalist, could believe in such things as the Cottingsley Fairies. Before the War, even such a stalwart figure as Msgr. Robert Hugh Benson had maintained a lively interest in addressing occult phenomena from a Catholic point of view; in the face of growing interest in these things after 1918, such disparate figures as Frs. Montague Summers and Herbert Thurston, S.J. attempted to apply the Church's teaching to them. This was the tradition in which Sir Shane was working.

But even more valuable than this and the stories themselves are his recounting of the attitudes of the Church Fathers and Medieval scholastics toward such occurrences. In common with these sources he divides haunting into those which appear to have an intelligence at work, and those which seem to be mere endless repetitions of a given occurrence—rather like a film inscribed upon the ether. The former he attributes to three agencies: a) demons masquerading as the dead; b) damned souls; and c) souls returning from Purgatory to impart information or ask for prayers. Sir Shane worked almost exclusively from English sources; there is no reference to such things as Fr. Victor Jouet's Purgatory Museum in Rome, with its collection of items literally burned by visitors from Purgatory, the similar items displayed in the treasury of Slovakia's Bratislava cathedral, or the work of the Austrian Benedictine Abbot, Dom Alois Wiesinger - his findings would be published a year later in the magisterial *Occult Phenomena in the Light of Theology*. Nevertheless, mention all of these disparate foreign sources would have backed up the credibility of Sir Shane's narrative. Even so, Sir Shane managed to create an immensely important book.

This writer first encountered *Shane Leslie's Ghost Book* back in 1978 in the shelves of the rectory library of the Church of the Assumption in Roswell, NM, where he was attending college at New Mexico Military Institute. The book made a huge impression on me at the time, and has been a sterling reference work whenever I have to write upon these topics. In this current era, when ghost hunting is big business on TV and the Internet, the need for this book has never been greater, and it is to be hoped that this new edition attracts a wide audience. Whether you are looking for theology or a quick scare, this is most certainly the book for you.

Charles A. Coulombe
Monrovia, California
31 July 2017
Feast of St. Ignatius Loyola
Lammas Eve

INTRODUCTION

THIS volume is the drift and silt of a life-long interest in ghosts. It is suggestive, not conclusive. Ghosts are illusionary mental rubbish or, if they represent faint links between this world and another, betwixt the dead and the living, they must be of considerable importance.

It carries no scientific value, save to show that religious and ghostly beliefs can get along very well together: that it is not impossible or uncomfortable to study psychical research while occupying a static view of revealed Faith.

As yet it is not possible to decide whether the uncanny, super-sensory, para-normal or ghostly (call it what you will) is really a department of the supernatural or an unknown branch of the invisible Nature around us to be distinguished as præternatural. As the Church requires no motion of Faith for or against ghosts, we incline towards natural explanations, if they can ever be reached.

Certain words of the late Provost of Eton, Montagu James, always sound in my ear, for they were the last and most solemn I ever heard him say. Shortly before his death I asked him what he really thought on the subject, since he had written better ghost stories than any man living. He answered: "Depend upon it! Some of these things are so, but we do not know the *rules*!"

Nothing wiser could be said about the whole phenomena of ghosts. Until thousands of incidents, apparitions, hallucinations and inexplicable happenings have been collected and classified, we shall never approach any kind of ruling.

It is, therefore, the duty (pious or scientific) of the life-wanderer to recall or, better, record at the time anything queer or uncanny on his way. Either its meaning may be resolved or it may be filed under the heading of what they call at Scotland Yard "unsolved mysteries," but with this difference that police mysteries have an earthly solution somewhere whereas ghostly events have generally no earthly meaning. We will suggest that sometimes they have a religious reference.

The first chapter is in the nature of an essay touching the whole question of the apparition or signalling of the dead to the living.

Belief or interest in ghosts is built up from a long succession of stories, hints, family odds and ends (chiefly odd), leaving a constant curiosity and sometimes a certain amount of acceptance in the mind.

Without possessing second sight (which I consider a gift like music or mathematics) I have always had a prepossession for the queer and all that raises unanswerable query.

Needless to remark that if everyone remembered or recorded whatever came untowardly in life, the amount of data would add considerably to the advance of psychical research. Some rules might be evolved or even a law governing the connection of the living with what is called the "other world."

The second chapter deals with psychical phenomena in the history of the Church. There is no getting away from these strange phenomena whether in the lives of saints or of perfectly ordinary people.

The third chapter touches the well-known and over-evidenced type of the uncanny called *poltergeists* or ghosts that make noises. They have been recorded *ad nauseam*. They are common in the records and materialistic in most of their symptoms. If they are spiritual at all, they are on a very low level. Father Rickaby the Jesuit compared them to "the little black things on the seashore, made for some purpose. Perhaps the Almighty in excess of creation-energy may have created similar things in the spiritual world."

Father Herbert Thurston, another Jesuit, devoted much thought and scholarship to the investigation of the poltergeist and three of his cases are recorded in his book on *Ghosts and Poltergeists* as first-class and first-hand examples, two from Irish sources and one from offices in the City of London (this was rather a famous one known as "Lister Drummond's Ghost Story." Lister Drummond was a devout convert).

My own contribution is the last word about a still more famous series of phenomena known as the "Coonian Ghost" which occurred in the county of Fermanagh in Ireland. Over many years recently it caused considerable interest and clergy did their utmost to investigate and to soothe the trouble. Eventually exorcism was declared permissible by the bishop, but the dean, to whom he delegated the office, preferred to leave it to the bishop. As a result, nothing was done and the unfortunate family, plagued by the poltergeists, left Ireland for America. I succeeded in collecting all the vital evidence of all the clergy who took a part in the investigations. As requested, I have omitted their names. It was as clear a case as could be found. There was no explanation and retreat was found the only method to deal with the unapproachable.

The Second Part of the volume is devoted to a collection of ghost stories out of the hundreds I have gathered. I believe that we would get somewhere by specializing all that reaches us out of the uncanny and placing them under careful classification, for instance:

Ghosts and Animals.
Ghosts of the Living.
Ghosts in Sport.

Celtic, Teutonic or Oriental types of Ghost.
Religious or anti-Religious Ghosts.

This small collection is intended to illustrate occasions between the Catholic Church and the ghostly. They are not necessarily spiritual and even less spiritualistic. Religion colours most of these stories, but some merely have occurred to Catholics or in Catholic surroundings. Whatever prohibitions mark Catholic life, the faithful are not forbidden to see ghosts or to believe in them!

Some, for those reasons, I have taken mention from old collections, although they are not evidenced or cross-examined in the way the Society for Psychical Research approves. Two collections of Victorian date are rich in Catholic ghost stories: Augustus Hare's *Story of My Life*, William Stead's Real Ghost Stories. One was a raconteur and the other a journalist.

Both books being out of print, I have helped myself freely. Hare was a raconteur of ghost stories in Victorian days in the style of Lord Halifax's ghost books, and, though undoubtedly he embellished his tales, he was an accurate recorder of facts and gossip as his Diaries have shown. Stead was the unbalanced Nonconformist prophet who out-Americanized American stunts in journalism. His interest in ghosts led him into credulous Spiritualism. He stampeded through the English-speaking world like the ghost of the great man he so nearly was.

With classification in aim I have been anxious to discover if Catholic ghosts yield special types (shall we say species of the genus?).

Apart from phantoms are poltergeists, which can show themselves pro-Catholic or anti-Catholic. Their action is so odd at times that Father Thurston laid down a special type called "ghosts that tease." Investigators feel that they have a lower sense of humour and enjoy making fun of holy things.

More interesting and more edifying types of occurrence can be briefly indicated:

1. When invisible or super-sensuous means are used from the other side to bring contact between the dying and the Last Sacraments.
2. When by apparition or signs or audible means deceased clergy obtain the saying of Mass (apparently unsaid) or the destruction of secret papers (affecting confessions).
3. When by sign or sound, visionary or mechanical, the dead obtain prayers from the living.

Type I is illustrated by the famous Oratory Ghost, which has already appeared in Lord Halifax's collection of ghost stories. In this case the real names and further details are given.

Though it has not always been possible, I have endeavoured to leave aside what is already authorized in the lives of saints or persons of supernatural life. The astonishing life of the Curé d'Ars or the incredible cures at Lourdes are a part of Church records. Both have roused deep interest amongst physicians and psychologists. I may quote from an unpublished letter which Frederic Myers, the founder of the Society for Psychical Research, wrote to a Jesuit scientist (6th June 1889):

My mind continues to be quite open to any facts or arguments on the matter and (as you will have seen) I absolutely *believed the evidence re* Louise Lateau at a time when Maudsley etc., were sneering at the lies told by Catholic physicians. I have also a strong belief on the reality of the phenomena accompanying the *Curé d'Ars*, though I am not clear at all as to the explanation. I do wish that scientifically-minded Catholics like yourself and Mivart (who at one time took a good deal of part in these investigations) would unite with us in discussing any supernormal phenomena which occur within the bosom of the Catholic Church. Of course, we cannot promise to agree but we can promise to listen respectfully, and to discuss without any sort of prejudice and to print any really evidential points.

Since the early days of the S.P.R. there has always been a small Catholic section like the third Marquess of Bute, Father Thurston and the Hon. Everard Feilding anxious to inquire and report. The relations of both Societies, the S.P.R. and the S.E.R. (*Sancta Ecclesia Romana*) have been similar towards ghosts generally (an attitude of prudent inquiry towards facts but of non-committal to any conclusion).

The S.P.R. was always tolerant and helpful in the days of Victorian materialism, and the mighty names which have figured in the Presidency, from Professor Henry Sidgwick to Lord Balfour, afford an assurance to those who still humbly seek, in the Scriptural phrase, to discern spirits.

To an American friend of mine, George Smalley, Lord Balfour once said: "There is nothing in political life which can be compared to the interest and profound significance of psychical research."

> So Man, who here seems principal alone,
> Perhaps acts second to some sphere unknown:
> Touches some wheel or verges to some goal.
> 'Tis but a part we see and not a whole.
> ALEXANDER POPE

Part One

ON GHOSTS AND POLTERGEISTS

I: "SOULES SOMETIMES APPEARE AFTER DEATH"
(DOUAI MARGINAL)

IT is generally supposed that amongst other restrictions Catholics (R.C.) are not allowed to believe in ghosts more than they are allowed to read an English Bible. This may be the popular belief, but incidents constantly break in contrariwise. Catholics, both priests and laymen, report ghosts or what are called "psychical phenomena." Many more notice them but say no more.

Similarly, Catholics read the Bible and stranger still translate it into English. The Church's prohibitions are conditional in both cases. The Bible, which can be perilous enough in places for the young and uneducated, may be read with careful notes and elucidations in the margins. A prohibition lies over any except guaranteed translations. Prohibitions more severely hedge the practice of necromancy or artificial communication with the dead. But the faithful, if endowed with supersensory power or "second sight," cannot be blamed for seeing or recording ghosts. They may be considered part of the paranormal, subconscious, and invisible world within and around us. If eventually they shall prove to be possessed by unknown natural laws, they will come under the heading of Science.

This will save much discussion with theologians. Moreover, if souls, presumably suffering the condition of Purgatory, appear after death, their ghostly manifestations must come under the Divine Permission. No one need quarrel with the sensible prohibition against attending séances, whether from curiosity or from a genuine belief in modern Spiritualism. Between the spiritual and the spiritualistic there is a wide gulf. The Western belief in Purgatory is instanced in the apparitions accepted by Gregory the Great in his Dialogues.

Psychical research presumes an agnostic type of mind, interested, and open to scientific experiment or religious experience. "*Ut videam*—help Thou my unbelief!" is the prayer of the true Agnostic.

Spiritualism covers a vast body of people who believe and practise communication with spirits of every kind. These spirits may be the souls of the dead, controls in the spirit-world, lower manifestations of the type called poltergeist or even demoniacal powers. The truly diabolical appears to be very rare, that is to say absolute manifestations of the Enemy of Mankind. The obsession of the type so often and clearly cured by Our Lord seem to point to hosts of lower spirits, in fact one sufferer alone accounted his as legion.

If there is any subject in the New Testament that is clear and practical, it concerns the casting out of devils. Today they carry medical rather than theological significance. Obsessions and possessions are a constant accompaniment of civilized life. Only medical skill on the one hand or a wise "discerner of spirits" on the other can exactly decide or guess whether the malady is of the mind or of the soul, proceeding from within or from an external influence. Today "possession is found to explain musical prodigies." The Bible gives two instances of the possession of animals: Balaam's ass and the Gadarene swine. Oliver Lodge thought "Balaam's ass may have been direct voice, if anything physical at all."

Some cases of possession may only be suffering temptations to take drink or drugs, their own lives or the lives of others. But there are cases where the impulse can be connected with an external site or spirit. In this case the

Church permits the dread service of Exorcism, but only under the strictest supervision and after evidential inquiries.

It is generally held that the bishop of the diocese must give permission and that the exorcist should be a newly-ordained priest, who presumably has no sin upon his conscience. The genuine demoniac is believed to have power to retaliate by revealing a knowledge of the exorcist's past life. In the case of Our Lord, of course, the obsessing spirit could only cry out in retaliation, "I know thee, who thou art, thou Holy One of God." And this was equally the experience of Paul and Silas when the woman "having a pythonical spirit" cried out to acknowledge they were the servants of the most High God! We are told that this woman made money for her masters: a kind of spiritual prostitution.

The financial side had already entered the profession which, indeed, has been reckoned the second oldest open to women in the world. This has been a consistent aspect of the modern pythoness commonly called a medium. This can come under the Law, but small fees seem reasonable.

The immense wave of Spiritualism which has flooded the world consequent upon wars and upheavals of thought and religion, is an excuse for this essay and collection of ghost stories appearing from the uplands of orthodoxy. In spite of the fraudulent and the delusive, spiritualism cannot all be rubbish. Gifted and successful mediums are few, but those who have been willing to submit themselves to the tests of psychical research have acknowledged a scientific basis. A greater number have claimed a religious background. Some have constantly received messages in a Christian and even in a Catholic sense.

The Anglican Communion claims many such, but the church officials have declined to make any pronouncement. In view of the evidence said to be submitted by devoted Anglicans such a pronouncement could only be favourable. Human evidence however is insufficient for a matter of doctrine or faith. Religion necessarily goes very much behind or beyond evidence.

Mediums have multiplied until many thousands must be earning the pythonical wage. But if only half a dozen have produced results which are credible to other than the credulous, it is sufficient to make a case for investigation. Not yet can we discern whether the invisible in human survival can be affected by unrealized laws. Of course, if one absolute case could be adduced of the spirit of a dead person clearly and unmistakably communicating with the living, the question, though not the answer, is clear—that is to say, the evidential fact could be accepted though the scientific explanation remained as distant as ever.

Catholics and the Christian majority believe in survival of the spirit but on trust. Faith and not merely Hope bids them to believe. The scientific spirit has asked for proofs of everything in the Christian creeds. Both Christian and scientist ask for proofs from the medium, the ghost-hunter and the spiritualist.

The Christian can refer to the vivid and startling chapter in the Old Testament which describes the appearance of the Prophet Samuel after death to Saul in the Cave of Endor at the invocation of a lady who would pass today as a successful professional medium. Even her control is mentioned as "a familiar spirit." Whether the passage is read in Vulgate Latin or Jacobean English, its strength and beauty are punctuated with shudders. The oldest of all ghost stories in history is warranted by Divine Writ.

The deep and insatiable curiosity felt by mankind towards that bourne, from which, Shakespeare says, no traveller returns, is satisfied with overwhelming power.

The account of Saul's last night on the mortal plane is worth study. The despairing king seeks a woman with a divining spirit because God has ceased to answer him in dreams or by word of the priests. In other words, the established clergy had failed him and the normal guidance by vision had left him. Guidance by dream was normal in Scripture for it enters both the Old and the New Testament as a divine agency.

The scene at Endor might occur under modern conditions. Saul went disguised to consult the medium who fears him as though he were an agent provoking her to enter a police snare. In his happier days, he had forbidden wizards. He assures her and at his command she raises the spirit of his ancient mentor Samuel from the dead. "I saw gods ascending out of the earth" is her terrifying description of what took place. Here, indeed, was a reality worth a thousand modern séances, for the dead prophet truly declared the terrible future awaiting Saul: "Tomorrow thou and thy sons will be with me." And so it befell, for they were slain in battle.

Sir Oliver Lodge gives the scientific summary:

> It is quite a good mediumistic episode. Orthodox people generally say that the witch was much astonished when Samuel really arrived. I don't see that. She cried out because she evidently got from him the identity of her sitter and immediately realized that she was in danger because of the police prosecutions which he had seen set on foot. However, she behaved very well to him and he got a good prediction.

The Douai version supplied careful notes. St. Augustine first took the view that a devil had taken Samuel's shape, but later, "he sayeth expressly: Samuel the Prophet being dead, foretold future things to King Saul yet living." Five proofs follow to the effect that "his verie soule appeared not compelled by the evil spirite but obeying God's secrete ordinance." This phrase concerning "God's secrete ordinance" will be found very helpful in the twilight between the two worlds, the middle condition which is neither of utter pain or bliss and can conveniently be called purgatory. In this discrimination of the next world's compartments Dante's geographical ecstasies are found too close to latitude and longitude, but logic and theology combine to adduce purgatory. Otherwise where are we after death? An ante-camera of "yellow light" is more than a convenience betwixt the stark choice of red and green, if we may so dub the Celestial-Infernal alternatives. The departed soul has a better answer than used to be given to the Biblical conundrum— "Where was Moses when the light went out?"

The soul is not in the dark, however far from Divine Light. The twilight of Purgatory is always a happy thought and lends itself to the hopeful propositions of Catholic teaching. Samuel may be thought to have risen from Limbo. The essential reflection that follows a reading of the Endor chapter is that the return of a spirit to earth is a possibility recorded in Scripture and is not outside Catholic doctrine. The story does not occur in the Lessons or in the Breviary, but it remains with convincing realism and uncloaked like the Song of Solomon in metaphors.

Whatever is the bridge between Seen and Unseen (phenomena being the term generally used to describe the latter passing into the former) the Divine Word has hereby shewn that there is such a bridge, and all psychical research is directed towards this bridge. As for such research, whether in the discerning of spirits or reception of signals from the other side, patience in a slightly critical, slightly reverent state of mind is recommended to the seeker. Much is allowable, but all things are not permissible. The Church forbids direct necromancy at what is described in Huysmans' most fearsome pages as the "Black Mass." The general practice of séances is forbidden, though there are priests and laymen who consider themselves permitted to be present at experiments in an unrevealed natural science. Sir Oliver Lodge was acquainted with such, as he mentions in his letters,

Ordinary Catholics are forbidden in the gross to have anything
to do with psychical research but exceptions are continually made.
For instance —— and ——[1] are Catholics, but they told me they
had arranged with their priests to be allowed a free hand.

The Decrees of the Holy Office say: "In all these
documents the distinction is clearly drawn between
legitimate scientific conversation and superstitious abuses"
(Edward Pace: *Catholic Encyclopedia*)

Amongst laymen this was certainly the case with the
Hon. Everard Feilding and amongst the clergy with Father
Thurston, S.J.

There is no need to pursue ghosts or to discern
unwilling spirits. If they are part of the invisible texture
around us, they can find their way to us. If they come to a
careful researcher, armed with some pre-knowledge, they
must take the consequences.

The object of this book is to collect instances of ghosts,
apparitions and messages from the other twilight world
which have come under Catholic cognizance or suggest
Catholic interpretations.

Ghosts or such manifestations need not be always laid
to the sinister or Satanic, as they generally were in the
Middle Ages. Even so, the records are packed with matters
mysterious rather than mystical, and with incalculable
happenings apart from the lives of saints.

Ghost stories have always been found useful in the
pulpit and collections were made with that purpose.
Preserved in the Lambeth Library is a wonderful collection
made by the Prior of the Holy Trinity in Aldgate. If such
stories had no other value, they made popular
reinforcement to the true Gospel read from the altar. They
corresponded to legends painted on the walls. They might

---

[1] The names are left blank for anonymity.

be true or they might not, but they were edifying. At least they often left a moral or the fear of God in the memories of listeners. Compare the wonderful frescoes that have been revealed on the walls of Eton College Chapel—ghost stories honouring the Blessed Virgin Mary.

In modern days, many stories have accumulated which have had not only a Catholic atmosphere but a religious design. Such a collection may well bear as a secondary title—*Deo permittente*—God permitting. The idea certainly occurred to Père Henri who mentions in *Nos Devenirs* that "sometimes the mysterious wishes of Divine Government permit a coming death to be revealed."

There are three different grades of religious ghost stories:

1. The warning dreams and hints of ghostly appearances which are enshrined in the Bible. These, naturally, have a value which the faithful cannot contest.
2. The astonishing psychic phenomena which are cited in the processes of canonization of saints. These, of course, have been severely contested during the process by a very necessary official of the Church known as the Devil's Advocate.
3. The ghost stories of old Catholic families, of the sacristy and the whispered *inexplicanda* which the practising clergy sometimes admit but seldom record.

The Church admitted ghosts in the Middle Ages or she would not have been so hostile when she suspected a diabolical origin. In dealing with them she certainly developed her own technique and used a special service for exorcism which has continued in the armoury of the Church although seldom used except in a hole and corner manner. At the same time, it is not necessary to suppose that either a demon or an angel, an evil or saintly spirit, is the invariable source of manifestations or messages from the other world.

Father Thurston commented on an interesting "Mediæval Ghost" (*Dublin Review*, April 1921), which had received varied treatment:

> Victor Langlois *de l'Académie française* has been delivering a conference upon it. It is a curious case of a soul supposed to have come from Purgatory to ask for prayers (A.D. 1323). Hauréau dismissed the story as pure fiction but Langlois shows that there is a remarkable historical foundation. Langlois thinks it was worked by ventriloquism, but I believe myself that it was a genuine visitant from the spirit world.
>
> ("The Ghost of Guy: a famous mediæval tale")

Ghost stories must be considered apart from all the terrible history of witchcraft (both in Catholic and Protestant repression). The exorcism of those possessed by demons is fair enough, but, as Pope Benedict XIV pointed out, these cases are few and far. That sage Pope rejected twelve of the accepted signs of possession. The whole subject has since passed to the study of hysteria and epilepsy. *The Roman Ritual* lays down certain specifics: (1) the knowledge of an unknown tongue, (2) knowledge of distant or hidden facts, and (3) the manifestation of a physical strength beyond the powers of the subject.

In primis ne facile credat ...
Nota habeat signa ...
Signa autem obsidentis dæmonis sunt ...

These obsessions occur true to type. We take one case out of many. From South Africa comes an authentic story of a girl in a convent who believed (rightly or wrongly) that she had sold herself to the Devil in return for the gifts which she coveted. The good nuns were prepared to take the speedy advance in her studies as a compliment to their teaching until she took to flying about the place without visible means of support. The bishop decided that these signs deserved Exorcism and proceeded to carry out the service not without prayer and fast. It took an hour to induce the girl to enter a church, where she confessed her ambitious attempt to deal with a malevolent power and collapsed happily *in sinu Ecclesiæ*.

To what extent can the theories and experiences of modern psychical research be connected with the mediæval? Does the Church allow ghost stories as a kind of occasional supplement to religious thought? Or may research be applied to such symptoms of an unexplored branch of Nature or sub-Nature, leaving the religious aspect out?

The Society for Psychical Research was an interesting product of late Victorian times. It was founded by Cambridge scholars like Frederic Myers, Professor Sidgwick and Mr. Gurney. It represented a reaction from a University of Mathematical "Wranglers," materialists and agnostics.

On 3rd December 1869, Myers during a star-lit walk at Cambridge asked Henry Sidgwick whether knowledge could be drawn from ghostly phenomena to solve the Riddle which Tradition and Metaphysics had failed to reach. How to unravel "the incurable incoherence of the Cosmos?"

Sidgwick drew him out of Agnosticism by encouraging a new line of research. German philosophy embraced the clouds. French called for logical negatives, but the dogged Anglo-Saxon seemed mentally suited to wrest the answer from cosmic phenomena. It was like wrestling with an unknown shadow: "I will not let thee go." So Myers broached his famous line of research. As a poet, he had opposed Shelley; as a philosopher, Darwin. The S.P.R. was founded in 1882. Myers came by way of Virgil and Plato, whose *Phædo* marked Myers' conversion to the soul's survival. In 1865, he had challenged the unknown by swimming the Niagara at night—an experience he hoped would resemble his view of death: "terrifying but easy and leading to nothing new." This incidentally was not Lord Desborough's experience as related to the writer. On the second occasion on which his Lordship swam the Niagara, he found himself in difficulties and preparing to fight his way out from waters which might easily have become fatal.

Myers' experiment recalls the suicide of the Greek philosopher, so sweet had Plato's *Phædo* made the prospect of finding survival on the other side.

The S.P.R. was received with perfect fairness until distinguished scientists like Sir William Crookes and Sir Oliver Lodge became persuaded that communications with a spiritualist world were possible. Criticism then became unfair, often refusing to examine what was becoming clearer in evidence. The Society took a perfectly reasonable position. They collected all ghost stories available from good sources, they investigated all, disproved some, and left others to stand on their evidence. Eventually it was supposed that laws in the spirit world might be disclosed. Science rather than Religion entered into the Society, which was joined by members of all Churches and agnostics of every grade. Myers and Gurney published a large collection of cases, from which those who wished could deduce, *The Survival of Human Personality after Death*. It has been remarked that this book may in time prove with Darwin's *Origin of Species* the most remarkable written in the nineteenth century.

The Society continues under a series of eminent Presidents to publish their proceedings, and attested cases of phenomena, which the laws of Euclid, Newton and Einstein ignore as outside their provinces or dimensions.

As yet no *Law* can be certified, only suppositions, hints

and comparisons collected towards a gradual certainty that natural and supernatural Laws are allied in ways not yet revealed to man.

If Science and Religion can be treated as separate tunnels, which cannot meet, or conflict, it is possible that psychical research is approaching an exploration which cannot be claimed as yet by either. It has not yet produced the laws necessary for a Science, nor has it added to the mystical or religious in belief or conscience. It remains a kind of Tom Tiddler's ground, which in the far future Science or Religion may suddenly demonstrate to be part of their demesnes. At present scientists like Crookes and Lodge have testified to phenomena much to their popular disrespect and discomfort. Obviously, they have experimented and taught ahead of their times and critics. Men of religion have often confessed to ghostly happenings in the course of their apostolic duties. Others have preferred to say little about happenings outside moral or pastoral theology. Priests who pay too much attention to ghosts find themselves discouraged in their careers in the manner in which Naval captains who log the Sea-Serpent in the course of a cruise are disapproved at the Admiralty. A Naval commander who saw such an unrecorded monster in peacetime might be expected to have delusions under more exciting circumstances of action. The evidence for Sea-Serpents has always been treated with the same mixture of levity and curiosity as ghosts. It is not surprising that the materialist cannot accept either unless brought to the laboratory in a bottle! "Some bottle!" may be properly remarked, but the phrase is metaphorical of the agnostic wish to touch, weigh, and analyse before credence can be offered. Incidentally, Professor Owen wrote that there was more evidence for ghosts than for one Sea-Serpent.

Two of my collected ghost stories from first-hand came from military sources. As one was a General and another an officer with a career lying before him at the War Office, we agreed that publicity might prove damaging. The General was a Brigadier when he adventured into the supernatural, but, as he was of Celtic and Catholic origin, his experience comes into the limited orbit of this book.

The best summary for those who find themselves on the side of ghosts in the manner that Disraeli found himself once "on the side of the Angels" may be given in a letter to the writer from Mgr. John Filmer (15th November 1945):

> I cannot see how Catholics can avoid believing in Ghosts seeing that the immortality of the soul is part of our Creed as well as the existence of Angels, good and bad. The only doubt in the minds of Catholics about any particular apparition must be whether it is really an apparition from the other world and if it is, whether it comes from God or the Devil.

It is interesting that modern Science has neither lessened the number of queer occurrences nor increased the old-fashioned skepticism. More scientists than ever are now prepared to be persuaded.

It would be interesting if the Census could divide the population into those who have seen a ghost and those who have not, as well as enumerate those who have suffered something queer enough to defy explanation. The difficulty is that *normal* and *paranormal* as scientific terms could scarcely be understood by the public. Nevertheless, if we are to get anywhere, we must postulate the *supra-sensory*.

A great many biographies and autobiographies contain a ghost story or at least one uncanny experience, but they are generally passed lightly over by the reader and no attempt is made to correlate them to other records. It is certain that for everyone told, a half-dozen are omitted, generally for the reason that ghost stories spoil the credence of serious biography. Those that are retailed are often garbled and lack the full evidence which could be taken at the time as well as the cross-examination which psychical research demands.

But the fact that they are often inaccurately told does not make it impossible for something of psychic interest to have occurred.

All such research is ungrateful. Immense trouble and time can be wasted. Further examination and prolonged study based on the first data can end in books of impressions (called evidence) and suggestions (called fancies). A few books collated with painstaking industry remain the classics of this kind: such as the *Adventure of two English ladies in Versailles*, the final account of *Borley Rectory*, "the most haunted house in England," and the Marquess of Bute's "Alleged Haunting of B," a shooting-lodge in Scotland.

The last-named, having been studied chiefly by Catholic investigators, comes within the scope of this book.

Ballechin (to give its true name) was a test case. Catholics interested in the investigation, apart from Lord Bute, included the Hon. Everard Feilding, a Jesuit, two Highland priests, and a bishop. The Jesuit, who brought the hauntings to Lord Bute's attention, "had done nothing but throw holy water about his rooms and repeat the prayer *Visita quæsumus.* ... It was natural that no result should be produced." Lord Bute read the Office of the Dead continuously in different places. He felt unseen presences that were "morosely unfriendly." Lord Bute reported the matter to an archbishop. Meantime the ghost of "Ishbel," a nun, had been seen by others. The climax came with the arrival of a visiting bishop. By that time there were ten Catholics present. Miss Freer, the hostess and editor of the book, describes the climax:

> There was Mass said this morning and as I knelt facing the window I saw "Ishbel" with the grey woman nearer the house than ever before. She looked pensive but as compared with last time much relieved.

It proved her last appearance, so from the Catholic point of view it was satisfactory. There was controversy and nothing was found proven, but it remained a model of careful research for future investigators.

It seems as though apparitions could be rarely vouchsafed but under the strict understanding of *Deo permittente*.

As Dr. J. M. Neale put the matter in his *Communications with the Unseen World*:

> It would rather seem that some strict law of the unknown state forbids such apparitions, unless, especially permitted. Doubtless well for us it is so.
>
> How it would alter the whole course of human existence, if such apparitions constantly took place. Whether they lost or whether they still retained their terror, it would hardly be compatible with worldly business that they should be permitted. In all such stories a superintending Providence seems most clearly manifest.

Père Henri in *Nos Devenirs* discusses the religious attitude to mediumship. The word medium in English has acquired such unpleasant insinuation thanks to Browning's unfair attack on Daniel Home in *Sludge the Medium* that it needs clearing and cleansing almost. Henri achieves this in one sentence when he ascribes "the higher mediumship and with what splendour!" to Jean Baptiste Marie Vianney, the Curé d'Ars. In him lay all the characters of true and veritable mediumship. It follows that "the little Thérèse of Lisieux was also a high medium." The life of such saints sufficiently illustrate what mediumship can be. On the films the Curé d'Ars has been vividly portrayed as "*le Sorcier du Ciel*." "Sorcerer" reads a little strong, but the "celestial magician" or "God's spiritualist" perhaps covers the truth. He was saint and medium in one and the two qualities increased and fortified each other. He enjoyed the best safeguard against errors connected with the profession of mediumship: "reasonable common-sense."

A medium in its simplest sense is a bridge, a connection, an invisible passage or influence between the Unseen and Seen, between minds disembodied and minds still in the body. The Holy Scripture can be a medium between God and man: likewise every true prophet and every saint, though the gifts which blessed and unhallowed mediums share do not necessarily appear in every saint's existence. It is difficult to think of prophets who do not possess the mediumistic gift of foretelling the future. Even the witch of Endor through the means of her control caused Samuel to relate the immediate future with agonizing accuracy.

Mediumship appears to be involved in natural but little understood laws. As a form of sub-science it is worthy of investigation and need not come under religious influence or prohibitions at all. When it is caught up by a saint or by some lower spiritism, there are phenomena of different kinds.

Ordinary mediumship connotes table-rapping, clairvoyance or second sight, automatic writing, healing. There are rarer and more difficult phases under the headings of Levitation and Materialization.

As for the evocation of spirits through table-rapping (the only case when a schoolboy would find some use for the First Declension *Vocative, Mensa*: O Table!), Père Henri says, "evidentially there is a fluid within you which mates admirably with the vibration of the wood."

In automatic writing "doubtless some invisible presence has added its activity to your own cerebral activity."

The healing emanation of the medium called "Healer" is a well-known faculty puzzling to the medical but acceptable to believers in the passage of vibration from the psychical into the physical.

The subject of Spiritualism is of some anxiety and even interest to Christian Churches.

With the Catholic Church it is more than a matter of warnings and prohibition. Spiritualists like Christian Scientists insist on being a distinct Church instead of a branch of Science. This, of course, is their right, but the Catholic Church has her own technique and views about mental healing as she has about communication by prayer with the dead. Lourdes and other shrines meet the case of healers and the would-be healed. For psychic manifestations, poltergeists, ghosts and dreams the faithful will find if not satisfactory explanation at least reasonable supposition, and in serious cases exorcism. The priests or confessors who can deal with these matters are limited. Priests like Father Thurston, S.J., who made a special study of all supranormal happenings, are very rare. His activities and findings must form a special chapter in every future book dealing with ghosts from the Catholic side. His posthumous *Physical Phenomena of Mysticism* opens a new era in Catholic research.

II: PSYCHICAL PHENOMENA IN THE CHURCH

D R. J. M. NEALE in *Communications with the Unseen World* (published anonymously in 1847) collected a number of spectral tales from writers of the early Church. Their titles qualify them for mention at the head of this chapter, such as:

"St. Gennadius rebuking a spectre which addressed him";

"St. Felix of Nola appearing when Nola was besieged";

"St. Eulogius of Alexandria seeing the living wraith of his Archdeacon Julian, who denied he ever entered where the saint believed he had seen him";

"St. Metas appearing and predicting coming troubles";

"St. Amatus comforting his mother by assuring her he was with the Lord";

"St. Cyprian confirming St Flavian in his coming martyrdom."

These might be described as ghost stories for Sunday reading: but at least they show that the Church accepts their possibility.

There is very little that is genuine in Spiritualism which is not paralleled in Catholic history.

Levitation, which in the case of Daniel Home, the greatest and most inexplicable of modern mediums, stirred many learned Societies and induced two peers of the Realm to make statements disparaging to the Law of Gravity, is abundantly shewn in the case of St. Joseph of Cupertino. If Spiritualists need a patron saint, they could not find a better. The Bollandists record his miracles in the *Acta Sanctorum*. St. Joseph lived in the first half of the seventeenth century. His moral life sufficed for the halo: for the Church discouraged him from miraculizing as much as possible. He was filled with such ecstatic joy on hearing holy names that he shouted and flew up and down, hanging pendulous in the air. Cardinals testified him to be genuine when he was brought to Rome, but his superiors found that his flights in church disturbed services. He said in a cardinal's presence that he shouted in the way that guns made a noise when they went off.

The Middle Ages were so rich in spiritual visions and religious excitements that the lesser or more secular kinds were seldom noticed though they were provided for by formula. At least there was a prayer against the spirit who makes noises, say, like a percussion cap (*spiritus percutiens*). Marie de France and Froissart record instances. See the story of this evil spirit in the Book of Tobias where the hero puts the murderous fiend to flight by spells. The formula dealing with this particular spirit will be found in the Benediction of bridal chambers and should accompany a devout honeymoon.

Mediæval legends are dismissed with a smile by the unbelieving and with a sigh by the faithful. The inexplicable was too often attributed to the Devil or the Blessed Virgin. Many stories may stand if the hagiological is translated into psychical terms.

Stories that were supernormal or præternatural were made acceptable to popular theology. They have descended the ages thanks to the beautiful treatment of artists on folio or fresco.

Apart from the Scriptural story of Our Lady there grew up a number of delightful stories of which the basis was often of a psychical nature. This is not to deny that the Blessed Virgin lent her aid in cases pertaining to the soul's salvation. Individuals tend to exaggerate their importance to the Powers of good or evil. Psychical research could better explain stories which, charming in their way, can embarrass the faithful.

For instance, amongst the popular miracles of Our Lady was the knight who halted to pray to her on his way to a tournament. On arriving too late, he found someone had successfully taken his place and disappeared. This could be explained as a case of *doppelgänger* which lies at the basis of the story of the erring nun who, after a gay life, returned to find *someone* in her similitude had taken her place all these years.

Many of these miracles in fresco were brought to light in Eton College Chapel by Provost M. R. James.

One scene corresponds to modern stories of the yearning soul who is suffered to attend Mass in dream or vision. A lady is allowed a vision of Mass in the presence of the Virgin herself and wakes to find she has retained the candle given her by the Virgin still in her right hand. Her left hand laid across her eye symbolized her slumber. ("Smallest details have a meaning explained by literary source." M.R.J.)

Perhaps the most striking of the Eton frescoes shows the lady who died without confessing a certain grave sin but was allowed to revive temporarily in order to receive absolution. The fresco represents her as a corpse, but also kneeling in her shroud to a monk seated in the chair of confession.

This appears to be an elaboration of what has happened in modern times when patients accounted dead have later been sufficiently restored to conclude their spiritual duties.

The Lambeth Library contains a mediæval ghost book, the MS. collection of *Petrus Londoniensis de visionibus* written soon after 1200 which has been catalogued and analysed by Provost James. The writer belonged to the Priory of the Holy Trinity in Aldgate.

The stories of visions, ghosts and the occult generally

in relation to religious life were no doubt intended to help preachers who were in need of arguments *in terrorem.*

Dr. James translates what the author has in mind in the preface beginning: "Since there are still some who believe that there is no God and that the world is ruled by chance and many who believe only what they see. ..."

The types vary from visions as they appear in the lives of the saints to the story of a veridical dream about some pigs told by John of Orpington to the author: "a very interesting tale simply told and quite probably true."

The famous ghost story *De spiritu Guidonis* comes as number 352. The English version appears in Horstmann's Rolle, vol. 11, 292.

Dr. James mentions each story as briefly as possible: "Monk dies suddenly, appears and relates deliverance by the Virgin."

"Nun of ill life appears to abbess."

With the Reformation the Catholic types of vision and "Miracles of Our Lady" drifted away from sight or memory. Witchcraft and a sorry kind of secular disturbance took their place. Covenanters and Methodists later were subject to the strangest happenings.

Poltergeists and ghosts were distributed amongst all the new churches. Eventually the Rationalism of the eighteenth century, the rule of Reason, cleaned up the miraculous and the paranormal until the historian Lecky pronounced that Church miracles had followed Hop o' my Thumb, but Andrew Lang added:

> Then Lourdes comes to contradict his expectation, and Church miracles are as common as blackberries. Mankind, in the whole course of its history, has never got quit of experiences, which, whatever their cause, drive it back on the belief in the marvellous.

The religious life in thousands of convents and

monasteries proceeds normally under direction and discipline. Only rarely from time to time there are troubles, psychical or doctrinal. Take the French convent of St. Pierre de Lyon which suffered the return of a dead sister who had fled, lived gay and died unhappily in 1524. Alas, no Blessed Virgin had taken her place until she could return on earth. From Purgatory she returned to haunt another sister. Her story was elucidated by the familiar modern process of raps. Incidentally "raps" were known long before modern spiritualism. Her body was brought back to her convent and buried with sacred rites. Exorcism was successfully said by Montalembert, who was Almoner to King Francis I. Finally, by raps the spirit intimated that her Purgatory of years had been reduced to days. A bright light was seen in the refectory whereupon the nuns, as well they might, retired to their chapel and sang the *Te Deum*.

The nun's name was Alix de Telieux and there was a literature of Tracts on the subject; on which Cardinal Tencin became an authority more than a century later. Sister Alix seems to have been lightly treated, but she manifested herself at a useful time, when Purgatory was being attacked in controversy.

Reginald Scot, who wrote the *Discovery of Witchcraft* in 1584, made some contemptuous references to Popish times: "Where are the spirits? Who heareth noises? Who seeth their visions?" It was clear that such phenomena were traditionally treated by offering the Holy Sacrifice. Scot suggested that such souls were gone to Italy to get Masses said for them. Likewise, that haunted houses were used by priests to uphold the doctrine of Purgatory. "Reginald Scot decidedly made his Protestant boast too soon," said Andrew Lang.

The most useful Catholic authority was a Jesuit, Petrus Thyrreus, whose *Loca Infesta* appeared at Cologne in 1598. He found that hauntings were reported of most different places and times. To steady his belief in ghosts with orthodoxy he quoted St. Augustine's story of a haunted house and of an Exorcism as given in the *City of God* (Book XXII, Chap. 8).

St Gregory in his *Dialogues* (Chap. IV, 39) tells of a deacon who haunted certain baths and was seen by a bishop.

What was good enough for the saints was good enough for this industrious Jesuit, who laid down haunting spirits to be of three kinds:

1. Diabolical.
2. Souls in damnation.
3. Souls in Purgatory.

He found, as the ages have found since, that certain sprites could be mild, truculent, or jocose! He thought that suicides, murderers, and murdered were liable to haunt.

But do the dead know they are haunting the living? It is possible that they are aware, but the tremendous authority of St. Thomas Aquinas favours the view that the dead are not aware of their own apparitions. Other spirits may be acting the part. In this, St. Thomas has touched one of the stumbling-blocks of modern Spiritualism. Manifestations may be genuine but not the manifester.

Thyræus is interested in the sounds made by spirits which he considers real, when all present hear them, but otherwise they may be what the Society for Psychical Research calls "auditory hallucinations." Thyræus realized that the loudest crashes need not be audible to all and there need be no real motion (or vibration) in the atmosphere.

Catholic ghosts are not always so useless and purposeless as the majority of spiritualized reflexes from the past, whether endowed with visible circumambient powers or capable of audible sound or of precatory or salutary motive.

Andrew Lang pointed out that Frederic Myers' theory

about the appearance of the dead belonged to St. Augustine:

> The Saint had observed that anyone of us may be seen in a dream by another person, while our intelligence is absolutely unconscious of any communication. Apply this to ghosts in haunted houses.

Old writers and modern students agree as to this "astral body": a happy and starry phrase which covers a multitude of apparitions.

Myers, echoing St. Augustine, writes of ghosts as "not conscious or central currents of intelligence—but mere automatic projections from consciousness which have their centres elsewhere"—but where? in Heaven or in Purgatory? Shakespeare thought of Purgatory when he designed the masterly scene in *Hamlet* and made Horatio appropriately swear by St. Patrick, the saint whom the whole of the Middle Ages, and not Ireland alone, associated with the Purgatorial condition.

There was the haunted house in Amiens which gave the devout Monsieur Leleu such trouble in 1746 that he called for Exorcism. The case was examined and attested by a Dominican Father, Charles Richard. It was clearly a poltergeist and the Bishop of Amiens licensed publication of the evidence after hearing the evidence of ten witnesses, "a number more than sufficient to attest a fact which nobody has any interest in feigning." There the good bishop hit the nail on the head.

Archbishop Temple, a sturdy and open-minded Anglican, said in his Gifford Lectures for 1934 that it was "undesirable that there should be experimental proof of man's survival after death." Faith presumably is preferable. "Experimental proof" is a displeasing phrase. The Church does not want (does not need) such in connection with the soul's survival any more than the chemical proof of transubstantiation demanded by the Anglican Bishop Barnes. Sir Oliver Lodge pointed out that neglect of psychic knowledge accounted for Bishop Barnes' flippant suggestion for applying chemical tests to consecrated species. These, though invalid sacramentally, could be distinguished by sensitives. The universe is not so simple as mathematicians think. For many unanchored minds, the appearances of Our Lord after death have become more credible through the work of the Society for Psychical Research. Frederic Myers believed that the evidence of the S.P.R. would enable the Resurrection to be believed in circles which would otherwise have abandoned the whole idea.

In excessively rare cases, God has permitted what amounts to an "experimental proof." The gospel symbol of such proof is St. Thomas the Apostle, whose bewildered doubts were realistically resolved by the risen Christ. In rare cases saints and sometimes sinners have received "experimental proof," but the general folk are better without it. St. Louis refused it, when offered a glimpse of the Holy Child in the consecration of the Host. The modern mystic, Abbé Lamy said: "If Our Lady were behind that door I would not ask her to come in. You have to pay for that sort of thing with the soul's tears."

The greater miracles are attributed to the power of the Creator to suspend the Laws of Creation. But do we know the Laws of Creation? Are there not inner laws of which we have the barest hints? These very hints we call marvellous or miracles.

Rationalism was rash enough to question miracles and consequently undermined herself. Materialism laid down a foundation upon indivisible atoms, but even the atom has now been fearfully dissolved. "Indivisible" can only be predicated now of the Holy Trinity. What are called gamma rays proceed from atomic explosion. By the time that di-gamma rays are evolved, the human race will meet the fate of Frankenstein.

The inquiry into the Psychical follows any inquiry into telepathy (accepted by some scientists). Telepathy seems a more personal or spiritualized form of the powers which have yielded television and the whole of wireless communication. These are inexplicable but regular in cause and effect. It is the irregularity in the Psychical that has repelled scientists.

Ether and vibrations go as far as research can suggest. What is ether? What is vibration? The symptoms are clear but the inner meaning is with God. Science, as we know it, cannot apply to the spiritual nor even to the paranormal, for scientists under the tradition of their Science are confined to the normal. Equally they are confined to the Natural, so that they need not be blamed if they stumble at the supernatural or paranormal.

The great Huxley, who said "Miracles do not happen," spoke within the cognizances of his own mind, but he had not the total view of what miracles are, nor how anything really happens. Plato worked out the web of Being and Becoming—what actually is and what is only happening— without passing the gulf between them. The Law of God is and the whole of the Universe of facts and things are just *happenings*, ourselves included. Neither believer nor agnostic has the right to say that what they cannot understand for that reason cannot happen. Miracles happen and so do ghosts! Whether ghosts are miracles or not, St. Thomas Aquinas accepts the apparition of the dead which he attributes to the special dispensation of God or else to the operation of spirits, good or bad.

The Curé d'Ars has been canonized by the Church. Apart from his asceticism and incredible powers of confessing and consoling souls, there was a continual clash with hostile manifestations. He combined the gifts of pastoral genius with those of a medium. He excited, attracted, and repelled influences which seemed set on destroying his parochial life. It is not too much to say that he lived with one foot in the next world and on the infernal side, over which he triumphed in the end.

The Abbé Lamy (whom the Church is far from considering for canonization) was a medium in the priesthood who attracted heavenly voices and visions to the earth. His life was not so diabolically straitened as the Curé d'Ars but he had his bad moments. He saw the Fiend as well as the Virgin Mary.

The interesting thing is that his powers often relayed his visions to others, who happened to be not necessarily in a state of grace but had their receivers ready (or as the Celts say were "feeling fey"). He shared a vision of Our Lady with his acolyte. Children robbing his orchard suddenly saw his Guardian Angel protecting him in the twilight, for he was half-blind. Carrying a statue of Our Lady to a shrine he found himself accompanied by certain dead villagers through a wood. At the Sign of the Cross, they disappeared.

The Church forbids the dead to be evoked, but there is nothing to forbid the dead making the gesture themselves, since it is clear that only by divine permission could they do so. A Catholic with the medium's gift has only to sit still to become aware of the passing spirits. The paraphernalia of a séance is quite unnecessary.

It may be as well to say that the enormous majority of séances, provided artificially, are far from achieving uniform success. The cases where the voices or thoughts of the surviving souls can be really identified are excessively rare. In a great many cases thoughts and memories and wishes are relayed and counter-relayed—with probably no deeper origin than is given to telepathy—with the result that the sitter is satisfied and the medium is genuinely pleased to think that she has consoled a fellow being by the use of a gift (which in nine cases out of ten she has not really got).

Later some theory must be offered how even this

secondary result occurs. It is sufficient to acknowledge that very few modern mediums have produced results which great scientists like Sir William Crookes and Sir Oliver Lodge have accepted as evidential. If they are what is supposed, their value is primary. Without giving them the adherence of faith they can be accepted as genuine on the evidence.

The Church is not interested in psychical phenomena unless connected with cases of canonization. The test of miracles is required of saints and the least memory or record of supernatural or paranormal doings is eagerly put forward by the votaries: in ninety-nine cases out of a hundred to be swept aside with devastating counter-questioning by the Devil's Advocate. But a few instances get through. As they say: it requires a miracle to prove a miracle in Rome.

Incidents in the lives of the saints do not count in a research and compilation of this kind. But the parallels between the religious and secular existence are clear enough. Psychical phenomena are evident in both categories. When they occur in the life of one who was otherwise a saint, they are attributed to angelical influences. Otherwise they are laid by the great authority Mgr. Albert Farges to human and diabolical counterfeits (*Mystical Phenomena*).

Diabolical displays are very rare, but common horseplay (we allude to poltergeists) is attributed to the Devil. A great deal of accidental but inexplicable occurrences seem to have human origins and in the case of Catholic ghost stories to originate from good influences. Many seem meaningless and foolish, coming under no ruling either of psychical research or mystical theology. St. Teresa in her *Interior Castle* wrote: "I would write a thousand foolish things that one might be to the point, if only it might make us praise God more." For her, evidently, one was enough.

Some of the saintly achievements are historical. Thus, Pius V looked out of a Vatican window and saw Don Juan of Austria's victory at sea over the Turks at Lepanto.

The secular parallel would be Sir John Macneill, whose second sight enabled him to see the capsizing of the *Eurydice* off the Isle of Wight from a window in Windsor Castle. At any rate, he was sufficiently aware of the catastrophe to call out "Luff, Luff!" as though actually on board.

Monsieur Olier, founder of the Sulpicians, saw a vision of the Venerable Mother de Langeac so clearly that he at once recognized her when they met.

St. Alphonsus Liguori while at Naples visited in spirit the dying Pope Clement XIV in Rome.

For the experiences of Monsieur Olier and St. Alphonsus there are many parallels. They are treated as spiritual telepathy and television by modern investigators. They do not appear particularly miraculous, perhaps not even supernatural: but præternatural and according to Laws of God which as yet neither physicists nor physicians of the soul have settled.

As for the dreams, visions and direct interventions by the Divinity in the lives of men in the Bible it is wiser and more reverent to lay them aside as "read"—in the manner that committees often allude to reports they cannot understand.

The phenomena attributed to the canonized belong to the Church, which has investigated, rejected, or discerned their veracity with sufficient care, leisure and scepticism.

Nobody is asked to put themselves or others up for canonization but Heaven help them if they do, for the Roman Court, sensitive to the frauds and delusions which have harmed the Church in the past, is quite remorseless. The least excuse is seized to disqualify a canonization, as so many dioceses and Religious Orders know to their cost. Visionaries and seers have a very poor chance. It took the

Evil One himself to bring the blessed Curé d'Ars to the attention of Rome. In his humble parish, the humblest of priests stood between the warfare of Darkness and Light so manifestly that his temporal and spiritual achievements satisfied the strictest tribunal in the Church. One wonders what the spiritual history of modern France would have been, had the general order of French curés been in his style. But Providence appeared to think that one was enough.

False prophets in the religious order, like their parallels in mediumship, give themselves away by mercenary or vanity motives. Even the excellent and well-meaning fall just as the angels fell—by pride, self-conceit, and even by delusions. The late Cardinal Ceretti gave us a most amusing account of a great Church benefactor in France who had died certainly as folk thought, *un vrai saint*, but unfortunately he thought so as well, for he left a considerable sum to further the process of his own canonization! This roused ecclesiastical laughter and he was considered to have knocked himself out in the first round, before the Devil's Advocate had entered the ring against him.

It is noticeable that when saints produce these phenomena, they do not require what can be called the paraphernalia—controls, trances, séances. They seem to pick up visions or messages naturally. St. Teresa's conditions must not be laid to hysteria but to ecstasy. An ordinary lover, loving in the supreme manner of women, might be accounted neurotic or erotic.

St. Teresa's states were sublimated and disappeared into a divine ecstasy. In physical proof of her sanctity she suffered the famous transverberation of her heart shewn in Bernini's most famous statue in Rome. That her human cardiac organ was found wounded after death showed that the spiritual power can affect a fleshly organ with visible results. Mind can mold matter.

This way appears materialistic, but a great number of Church miracles and a certain class of ghost story come under this heading: that is, visible physical effects are left by the Unseen. The Unseen may be out and out divine or diabolical or only of that neutral quality which comes under divine permission though nor from direct divine emission. Briefly, such as can be studied in a category of Catholic ghosts.

All curative miracles from Lourdes downwards are instances of the physical cured without physic: operative healings without operations. These have been dealt with so extensively that there is no need to touch on the apparitions of Our Lady at Lourdes or Salette or on their results. The scope of our collection covers minor or accidental occurrences not leading to public worship and veneration.

We are constantly confronted with hauntings where priests have been summoned to lay the ghost. If ghost or wandering soul it is, the saying of prayers or Masses is the proper course. In the case of obsession or diabolical intervention the Church has provided Exorcism.

Prayers and holy water have a soothing effect in the one case, but rather tumultuous resistances in the case of the other.

Ghost-watching should be carried out seriously or not at all. John Marquess of Bute patronized a famous investigation where scientific researchers and Catholic priests took part at different times. Lord Bute himself read the Office of the Dead in different rooms, as I have already mentioned, and took an intense interest in all that was recorded by a succession of picked visitors.

The Alleged Haunting of B[allechin] House appeared from Lord Bute's hands in 1899. He himself was a Vice-President of the Society for Psychical Research and made inquiries concerning the second sight of the Catholic Highlanders in N.W. Scotland. He favoured research with due precautions and proper guidance. He never doubted that communication was permitted between the living and the dead and noted in his Diary: "My study of things connected with the S.P.R. has had the effect of very largely robbing death of its terrors." (*Memoir* by Abbot Hunter-Blair.)

The proper mood for a priest on another such occasion may be extracted from a letter from Fr. Cyril Martindale to myself:

> There had been several attempts at suicide on the premises and an alleged Sense of Evil in one particular room which (also allegedly) much alarmed a hefty Rugger player ... I was asked to go and stay there, so I did, not feeling at all the right person for such enterprises. I sat up in the room, with a breviary, patience cards, my rosary round my neck, a thriller, and positively steaming with Holy Water. The Horror was alleged to show itself at 2 a.m. I stayed there till after 3 in an ever worse temper and nothing whatsoever happened to me then or later. Next day I blessed the various rooms, calling such spirits as might be about by the most insulting names and then apologizing in case they might be quite nice ones and the Evil (if any) in the people they met and not in them ...

More seriously Fr Martindale wrote:

> I incline to think that God speaks directly to what they used to call *la fine pointe de l'âme* that is *under* anything visual or audible, and that the recipient instantly clothes this in ideas and then imaginations and then words, and that God, if He pleases, prevents the recipient from making any substantial mistakes.

Father Martindale has addressed the S.P.R. on the apparition of Our Lady at Fatima.

St. Thomas Aquinas says: *Quod mortui viventibus apparent qualiter cumque vel contingit per specialem Dei dispensationem ... et est inter divina miracula computandum.* That is that the ghosts of the dead appear by divine dispensation and this amounts to miracle. The converse would be that those which did not come by divine dispensation were not due to miracle, i.e. to some common natural law (as yet undiscovered by human) or to diabolical agency.

It may be suggested that many ghosts do not come at all by special divine or diabolic interposition but are already there in the ether, left by the dead, but liable to be galvanized by those who have moments of "second sight" into these floating photographs. These may be awakened or developed by certain powers of the mind or through cumulative impressions in certain families. They are frightening but not necessarily supernatural, as we have not yet discovered the limits that the natural can reach.

The dead can only know what is happening to the living by *grace*, says St. Thomas Aquinas, and who can interpret the limits of God's grace?

Purgatory is indeed a word as blessed as the old lady found Mesopotamia, and it lies also between two rivers— to speak in metaphor—the River of Life which empties itself into heaven and the River of Hades or Acheron, which winds into the outer darkness: theologically Hell. Spirits in Heaven or Hell cannot be expected to make appearances on earth. The common-sense view was once established in a memorable dialogue:

> BOSWELL. This objection is made against the truth of ghosts appearing: that if they are in a state of happiness, it would be a punishment to them to return to this world; and if they are in a state of misery it would be giving them a respite.
>
> JOHNSON. Why, Sir, as the happiness or misery of embodied spirits does not depend upon place, but is intellectual, we cannot say that they are less happy or less miserable by appearing upon earth.

When Boswell mentioned the concern that Dives felt for his dead brethren, Johnson agreed that, if not metaphorical, it was to be supposed that "departed souls do not all at once arrive at the utmost perfection of which they are capable."

This hints of the middle country of Purgatory. Johnson agreed that it was not wrong to pray for the souls of deceased friends.

III: POLTERGEISTS

P OLTERGEISTS—noise-nuisance ghosts—are as great a nuisance in general as in private. The accounts of their endless, low-level, malicious, maddening, unexplained disturbances lead to no progress in spiritual or spiritualist knowledge. They are too much of a muchness, but as long as the divine permission remains under which they act, unchecked, every instance is worthy of investigation as well as the taking of evidence and pigeon-holing for reference.

The Church is not always successful in dealing with the poltergeist. Stones are thrown, crockery smashed, and manifestations of gross materialism are made from the lifting of pianos to the brutal hurling about of coffins in closed vaults.

Amid much literature I take Dr. Hereward Carrington's *Historic Poltergeists* for a few cases of Catholic interest.

The Cideville case which took place in the house of the Parish Priest, 1850-51. (*Proceedings*, S.P.R., Vol. XVIII, p. 454.)

In 1867 Mr. F. A. Paley, a famous Greek scholar of Cambridge and a Catholic convert, reported *in Notes and Queries* that coffins had been disturbed in the vaults of Gretford near Stamford.

In 1907 the Jesuit Fathers reported poltergeists which they had observed at first hand in Jamaica.

In 1913 Sister André de Marie Immaculée described stone-throwing and the like from India. It was properly exorcised (*Revue Meta-psychique*, September-October

1928).

Father Thurston became a receiving area for such information, generally from perplexed Catholics but also from Spiritualists, who respected his immense knowledge (chiefly of the Middle Ages) as well as his theological common sense.

Among his papers is a note from a Dominican who reported in 1937,

> ...a well authenticated case occurring in Grenada (B.W.I.) two years ago. The usual stone-throwings on several occasions and finally a house mysteriously burnt down. The phenomena well-witnessed by some hundreds. ... The magistrate's verdict on the house-burning stated that no cause of the fire could be traced.

When poltergeists take to arson it is really too much, but there are many more cases than are ever recorded. Pyromaniacs, who unconsciously set fire to buildings, are the accompaniments of such outbreaks in the same way that girls reaching puberty of a certain type so often offer mediumistic channels to the stone-throwers and mysterious "voice productions."

Two instances passed my tracks in a lifetime which could be attributed to this unhappy cause. There was a fatal fire at Eton College in 1903 which was repeated when the unconscious "fire-carrier" was moved to another House. He was, of course, acting under paranormal influences.

While staying as a guest of the late Harley Granville-Barker in his Devonshire home I had the astonishing experience of facing two fires during one weekend. And a third had preceded them. It caused all the nervousness, dismay, and bewilderment these unpleasant spirits endeavoured to bring about. It was eventually brought home by detectives to a weak-minded page-boy. The poltergeist used the easiest way of making flames. An accompanying disturbance was a motor-horn which hooted in a locked garage of its own accord.

It is noticeable how often rectories and the abodes of clergy are subject to these happenings, from the Wesley family in Epworth Rectory to Borley Rectory, "the most haunted house in England," which perhaps under the pressure of too much investigation burst into flames on its own account.

Ireland, like every other country, has been subject to poltergeists. I will only recall a few locally.

Sir William Barrett (a President of the S.P.R.) investigated a lonely farm at Derrygonelly near Enniskillen in Fermanagh, a parish I know well. Mental questions were answered by raps and the number of fingers extended in his pocket was correctly given. (*Proceedings*, S.P.R., XXV, pp. 390-95.) The same volume gives Sir William's investigations of the Enniscorthy Case on the testimony of first-hand witnesses. He described,

> ...how at Derrygonelly I saw a large pebble drop apparently from space in a room, where the only culprit could have been myself and certainly I did not throw it and how at Enniscorthy in 1910 a heavy bedstead lacking one castor, with young men sleeping in it, was dragged right across the floor.

Irish poltergeists are inclined to trouble sleep. I can add one small instance. On June 1910, I performed the Pilgrimage to Lough Derg with two young Catholic students, Mr. Smyth and Mr. Moynagh. We did the pilgrimage with fervour and returned walking from the lake to the village of Pettigo in Donegal. As the village was on family property, I suggested we should sleep the first night (after two without much sleep on the Island of St. Patrick's Purgatory) in the Agency. Here I slept as I had often slept in the past, the sleep of the just. But my companions, who had deserved every consideration from Morpheus, were troubled and tossed and torn by a ghost who stripped the bedclothes from them. By the morning they had not slept a wink. They were considerate enough to avoid telling their host, but they confided the night's work to Mr. Flood, a reputable publican, who was certain that they had encountered the Protestant spirit of Mr. James McCullagh, who had long been Agent but had died two years previously. Poor James's feelings can be understood at finding Catholic pilgrims in his beds. But the Parish Priest at home told me that, before they parted for ever in this world, the old Agent (who had a compassionate record in the 1879 Famine) had asked him to do his best for him in the next world. Smyth felt the bedclothes stretched over him and then a foot which descended between him and the bed. Moynagh said the clothes had been rolled up over him like the drop-curtain in a theatre.

Do spirits object to a change of doctrine in the buildings they know? The late Lord Granard told me of a Covenanting ghost in Lord Loudoun's Castle, which gave trouble whenever there was a Catholic guest like Lord Granard staying in the Castle. The hammerings would allow no sleep or rest.

My old friend Monsignor Henry England had a strange experience at the Church of the Holy Apostles in Pimlico. He had converted a Nonconformist Chapel to Catholic usage. He lived on one side of the building with a community of Franciscan nuns on the other. One night there was a noise as though the planks were being raised in the chapel. The Monsignor peered out of his door and saw the frightened nuns looking out of the other. Cardinal Hinsley gave permission for the service of Exorcism which had no effect on the noises. Exorcism is aimed at Satan and a poltergeist is on a lower or say less sinister level. It may have been caused by the spirits of ministers who had returned to the scene of their preaching and found a change in doctrine. Can spirits, who fail to express themselves, cause the poltergeists to take their place?

It is curious to study the reactions of poltergeists to sacred objects. At Derrygonelly leaves were torn out of an open Bible. A lamp sprinkled with holy water was taken away. Passages read from Scripture were received with knockings loud enough to drown the words but gradually ceased entirely. In other words, both Churches were superficially baffled.

Case 1

THE COONIAN GHOST

THE poltergeist at Coonian near Brookborough, County Fermanagh, dates from 1913-1914. Father Hugh Benson had promised to come and investigate but died in October 1914. It was at different times investigated by three priests, from whom I collected the following notes. Incidentally I learned that Cardinal Moran, when Bishop of Ossory in the seventies, sent three priests to investigate two nieces of his own in Kilkenny aged 14 and 15, who became subject to noises and obsessions. These all ceased after Exorcism. In the Coonian case Bishop McKenna of Clogher, deciding it was diabolical, deputed Dean Keown to exorcise it, but the dean withdrew leaving it to the bishop. As in the Derrygonelly case and so many others, bewildered and innocent girls, touching puberty, became unconscious mediums enabling mischievous forms of spirit life to manifest themselves.

There was really no ghost-origin dating from real life except a rumour that an old pensioner had been murdered there on the day he drew his pension. This may have opened the way for the poltergeist, but the only ghost described was very unlike an old pensioner. A man had entered the house over-early in the morning and while waiting at the fire saw a ghost "come down like a ball of wool in a black bag by the trapdoor and coach round the floor."

The house had passed from Burnsides to Corrigans, to

Sherrys and Murphys, under whom troubles began. The Sherrys occupied it one night only, but kept quiet and sold it six months later.

When the Miss Murphys lay by the fireside, the pillows were torn from under their heads. A priest told me that he heard *it* snoring in the dark and sitting on the bed it felt like snakes moving under him, and when a light was lit, a human bulk was seen to collapse under the sheets and then develop a new swelling while the snoring started afresh.

It showed Protestant hostility to holy water which seemed to infuriate *it* for it played back the tune of "Boyne Water." He placed the sacred Pyx where there was a noise, which sank underground but still sounded from the depths.

He investigated more than fifty times. *It* came down like the sound of straw in the air. *It* operated on a bed with testers in a corner, where three or four young girls up to eighteen slept. Once he saw a human form raised under the sheets of an empty bed until *it* collapsed. He described *it* as like an animal moving underneath. He felt fear when *it* was spitting at him or lapping like a dog or escaping under him on the bed. He always addressed *it* as "Johnny." When *it* was asked to play "The Soldiers' Song," the tune came in taps.

Another priest described going there one night and finding a mother and two girls sleeping on pallets round the fire away from the haunted room. The moment the children returned to bed, there was a sound like a kicking horse. The bedclothes were thrown across the room. He held the children by their four hands with one hand and laid the other one over their feet. When the phenomena continued, he was convinced the children could not have produced them. At the suggestion he made that *it* came from a far distance—from Hell—there was a big hiss. He stood with his hand on the bed and challenged *it*. There was clearly something like a rat moving around his hand under the clothes. He had a shock and the feeling of an eel "twisting round his wrist but no farther. *It* did not dare touch his *consecrated hand*! He remained there till four in the morning.

A canon of the diocese told me he went about sixteen times. Once he heard a musical noise in the ceiling. He said: "Perhaps *it* will whistle." *It* did whistle. There was certainly an intelligence working behind and he was as certain of the ghost as of his being alive. "*It* fooled us as it was contradictory and gave nothing definite about itself. Holy water was used copiously. *It* was vexed and fled more and more along the wall while the knocking became more pronounced. Mass was said in the kitchen where henceforth relief and sleep became possible for the Murphys, When the children sat on a stool, the noise continued round them. When I cracked my thumb, it cracked louder. We asked for nine raps for *yes* and they came. They tried it in Irish and Latin successfully. They asked: "How many of us were born in County Monaghan?" Answer correct. They asked: "Could you put the dog from under the bed?" The collie came out dancing mad, with fire from his eyes.

A famous horse-dealer invoked *it* in the presence of visitors from England. It answered accurately with raps how many of them had been born in Ireland. "How many horse-dealers present?" *It* thumped under his chair. The first time he investigated he left a pony trap outside. The lights were mysteriously put out and the pony was terrified. The driver said someone had passed several times in the same direction but never returned. Later a teacher had his bicycle lights mysteriously put out.

"Well, what was the end of it all?"

The Parish Priest was weak and nervous about the ghost. The clergy were divided in opinion. The old ones kept away, but the young curates leaped in where angels might fear to tread. The girls were expected to produce results every time and did so, for two curates believed they had caught them in fraud, when the ghost was not sounding. The girls were avoided at crochet class for no one would sit by them. When they took refuge in neighbours' houses, *it* always followed them. As the Parish Priest would not believe them, they marched to his house and after that he believed, for it came down his back!

The canon later wrote to me that as I was writing a book on the subject I should have all this information following (12th November 1944):

It was noised abroad that the children themselves, three of them, ranging from 9 to 13 years, were making the noises on the wood at the head and bottom of the bed. On this particular evening there were nine or ten in the room, the knocking all around fairly vigorous, and although none of us there believed that the children were knocking, I suggested that two men in the room should come over and hold the hands and feet of the children so that a false rumour should be disproved. They did so. I sat on the bed-stock also. The knocking continued as usual but much more vigorously, for ten minutes, when suddenly the two men rushed away saying they were being punched and pushed off the bed. They would not return. I was not pushed away from the bed, but something moved close to my back up and down the length of the bed. I was not afraid, and remained for five minutes or longer. This killed the rumour that the children were making the noises. It was also rumoured that some of the family read bad books and had the "Black Art", etc. This was quite untrue.

I think it was the same night that a sheep dog belonging to the family came into the room. I put him under the bed and said something like this. "Whatever is there, I would ask you, if you have the power, to put this dog out." Suddenly such noises, all around the bed, as never were heard, burst out and frightened us all, with the result that the dog rushed out, nearly knocking me down on his way. No inducement could get him, freely, to come into the room afterwards.

Now I am going to relate the most remarkable incident I experienced during the whole time I spent in Mrs. Murphy's.

Our usual course, whether Father S. and I went together or singly, was to go before the family retired. You may remember that I told you that when the first "manifestations" were made, the Bishop, Dr. McKenna, was notified about them. He told Father S.

to say Mass in the house. There were three apartments in the house. He said Mass in the kitchen, which was the middle one, and as this was done at a very early period, the children could, from that time, sleep undisturbed in the kitchen. When Father S. and myself visited the house we usually had the children put in their own bed, which was in the room to the right as you entered. Sometimes the knocking, etc., would commence vigorously as soon as they would go to bed; otherwise less vigorously, perhaps very mildly, or perhaps not at all. Sometimes it did not start for about an hour after they went to bed.

On this particular night, there was no noise in the children's room although they had been in bed for more than an hour. The rest of us were sitting around the kitchen fire chatting when I asked James, unknown to the others (he was an intelligent boy of about 25 years), to get a candle and matches. We went to the other room on the ground floor where no one was sleeping. This was a fairly large room; two windows with blinds drawn, a bed covered with a white quilt, also some chairs. We stood in the middle of the room in almost complete darkness, and listened. For five minutes all was silence. Suddenly we heard the tramp diagonally across the room upstairs, of something like the footfall of a fairly large dog or sheep. It continued. We listened. James said there was nothing in the room above but some chaff and a bundle of straw. The room was being used as a barn and was reached by stone steps on the outside at the gable end. Leaving James where he was, I took the candle and matches, went out, up the steps and stood at the door for a few minutes. I then walked round the room three times. The barn was as James described it. I heard or saw nothing. I returned to James who told me that the "tramp of the dog" had continued all the time. James then went to the barn, and I remained below. It had the same result. Nothing above and "the tramp" of the dog heard below.

Very soon after we were standing together in the middle of the room. Something that I cannot describe and did not see, rushed down, practically touching us, and went into the earth. For the first time we were really frightened, but soon we immediately noticed that the tramping above had ceased. I then said to James that it was breaking day and to pull up the blinds. He did so. Day was dawning, as it was summer time. We clearly saw the room and immediately noticed, although there was no wind blowing in the room, that the bed-clothes were moving up and down fairly fast, especially in the centre of the bed. I actually went and held my hand over the bed and tested the matter for two or three minutes.

After that, we went to the kitchen, where the family, Mrs. Murphy, her two grown-up daughters and I think Father S. or possibly some neighbour were chatting. We had been absent about half an hour. We told them what had happened. They wondered, took their chairs and stools, came to the room. The movements of the bed-clothes were gradually getting more pronounced, vigorous, and defined. The whole thing resembled the form of a person lying diagonally across the bed in his or her death agony. The centre where the clothes were heaving most was where the chest would be. Soon we could hear the heavy breathing, the gurgling in the throat, the symptoms of pain. It resembled what country people would call "a hard death." From the time they came from the kitchen the whole death-scene occupied ten minutes at least. Finally, the movements and death-symptoms ceased and the room was as silent as the grave. I only saw this scene once, but heard that there were further such manifestations later on, but I can't vouch for their truth.

Soon after this scene I was transferred from Maguiresbridge to Fintona. But I heard afterwards that old people from the locality said that in the "olden days" an occupant of the house hanged himself in that room. I cannot vouch for this.

Now I come to item No.3 which is as strange in its way as anything else recorded. Some time near the end of my time as Curate of Maguiresbridge I took it into my head that *possibly* other members of the family were "affected" as the people said, and that *possibly* one of the full-grown daughters, Annie aged about 20, or Mary about 22 years, was affected. So I went in the middle of the day, alone, saw Mrs. Murphy and asked her to tell me the whole truth about the matter. She told me that Annie was "affected" and that it did not develop until Mass had been said in the kitchen. Being a big girl, the mother said, and I agreed, that we should not let it be known publicly. The mother sent to the field where she was working. She came in. I brought Mrs. Murphy and herself to the bedroom on the right where there were so many "manifestations". I told her to stretch herself out on the bed and then threw a rug over her. To my great surprise from the ceiling above the door which led into the room from the kitchen, a peculiar *rush* immediately came, until it reached half-way down the wall and then turned at right angles until it reached the head of the bed where the girl was and then the knocking commenced most vigorously. I asked her to rise. She arose, and immediately the same rush, distinctly audible, rushed back, turned at right angles and into the ceiling.

I then asked Mrs. Murphy to get into the bed. She did so and there were no manifestations. I asked Annie to go again. She did so, and whatever came, came by the same route and departed as before. I tried Annie twice more with the same result, and also Mrs. Murphy with a negative result. This to my mind was very strange indeed. Any person in the room could hear the comings and goings as distinctly as the ticking of a Grandfather's clock, but the noises were five times louder on this occasion.

The final item is—soon after the manifestations commenced Fr. —— was out on a sick call[2]. He was passing Murphy's, on returning, and had the Blessed Sacrament with him. The noises were great around the bed that night. Fr. —— and some of the neighbours were in the room. So, after lowering the light, Fr. —— —— took out the Pyx and made the Sign of the Cross with it, over the bed unknown to the others. He had no sooner done so than all the noises imaginable were made before the evil spirits departed, and did not return that night. The people in the room threw themselves on their faces and were terrified thinking Fr. —— was about to be attacked.

I heard the story of the terrible noises afterwards, and of what they believed was an attack on Fr. —— from some of the people who were present. They did not know he had used the Pyx.

This is a summary of all my experiences.

It remains to be added that the family retreated to America, where they were no more troubled. The gallant clergy, who made such constant efforts on their behalf, seem to have been the worse for it. One priest had a nervous break-down, another spinal meningitis and the third facial paralysis.

On the whole, their bishop was justified in his diagnosis of diabolical origins. So much was said and rumoured that I am glad to have interviewed the three priests and obtained the most trustworthy evidence concerning the "Coonian Ghost."

No doubt, matters would have been more successful if the Exorcism Service had been performed as the bishop

---

[2] The priest's identity is anonymous.

wished, but it was too serious a matter to lay as a command on any member of his Chapter. It was not a ghost but a poltergeist obsessed by truly Demoniacal powers.

The Curé d'Ars was perpetually assailed by such poltergeists between 1824 and 1858. Far from gaining the mystic peace of the contemplatives he found himself definitely at war with these evil manifestations. Whatever the persecutions which he endured, he found they were always followed by consolations. Incidentally the approach of great sinners to his confessional was always heralded by the fierce attacks of baffled spirits.

Case 2

THE PLUMSTEAD POLTERGEIST

by The Rev. Edmund L. Loman

I went to Plumstead on the 3rd August 1918, three weeks after my ordination. Nothing was further from my mind than I should have my first experience there of the præternatural. Indeed, I was occupied with very different thoughts: the new work I was about to commence, and how I would shape up to it; what my Rector and fellow curates were like; how the people would receive me. Nor did a very ordinary smallish modern house like the Presbytery in any way predispose me to expect a ghost. These are important points in determining the objectivity of the phenomenon.

One evening, a few weeks after my arrival, I was kneeling at the back of the church while my fellow curate, Father John Keogh, was giving Benediction. I noticed a very rough-looking man standing there with his cap on, and looking-about him in a way which aroused my suspicions. I went up to him and asked him what he was doing.

"I'm only listening to the music!" he replied.

"You had better do that with your cap off," I replied. He muttered something to himself and slunk off. What has all this got to do with the ghost?—Read on.

That night I woke up in bed, and as I lay there I heard a dull thud, thud, going on somewhere down below. I turned over and tried to get to sleep again, but the noise persisted and became, if anything, a little louder. I sat up and listened, but could hear nothing, so I settled thyself down to sleep again. No sooner was my head on the pillow than the noise started again. Once more I sat up; and once more it stopped. And so it went on for some time. Suddenly I thought of that man in the church. That was it. He was trying to break in the church door with some muffled instrument. I got up, crept down the stairs and felt for the hall-light. I switched it on and made for the front door expecting to see a crouching figure through the glass. There was nobody there. I then heard a noise below in the kitchen. I went down, and as I put on the light, saw the pantry door move slightly. "Now I've got him," I thought, and nerving myself for a tussle jerked open the door. Out shot the cat! Both relieved and annoyed I went back to bed. The noise started again, but I eventually got to sleep.

The next morning at breakfast I told Father Keogh of my experience. He looked at me for a moment and then said:

"Well, you might as well know now, that's it."

"What?" I asked.

"The ghost."

I burst out laughing. "You can't pull my leg as easily as that."

"I'm not pulling your leg. It's a fact. Father McCarthy and I have purposely told you nothing about it, but now you have found it out for yourself there is no point in keeping silent about it any longer."

I remained very sceptical, but he assured me it was so, and warned me that now the ghost had introduced himself to me I should probably hear more from him! No one had ever seen him, only heard him; and the strangest thing was that sometimes only one would hear him; sometimes two; and sometimes all three of us.

Two main incidents remain very vividly in my mind to-day, although it is nearly thirty-two years since they happened.

On one occasion, when I was burning the midnight oil,

I was last up to bed: The others were sleeping peacefully
while I went into the bathroom to clean my teeth. All of a
sudden, I heard quick heavy steps coming up the stairs and
on to the landing where the bathroom was situated. My
nerves went. I dropped my toothbrush and fled to my
bedroom, locking the door! Not another sound. When I had
calmed down, I was thoroughly ashamed of my cowardice,
and made up my mind that if another chance came my way
I should not fail a second time. Of course, my confréres
were highly amused when I related the event to them the
next morning. *They* had heard nothing!

A few days later I was sitting in my study saying my
Office at about 10:30 p.m. The stairs came down by the
side of it, ending just short of the door. Without any
warning those same quick heavy steps came running down.
I jumped out of the chair, rushed to the door, and pulled it
open, wondering what I was going to see.—Nothing! I
went across the hall and knocked at the Rector's door.
Father McCarthy, later Canon, was the occupant.

"Did you hear him?" I asked.

"No."

"He's just run down the stairs. I determined not to miss
him this time, so I pulled open the door, but there was
nothing there."

"It's just your imagination. I didn't hear anything, and
I am sure I would. Rarely let's me alone."

"It's not my imagination," I protested, "I was saying
my Office and not thinking of the ghost at all."

"It's all your nerves," he replied. "Go back and
continue your Office, and try not to think any more about
it. You'll go to pieces if you do."

Much annoyed at this attitude I returned to my room
and resumed my Office.

Shortly afterwards there began that continuous muffled
thud, thud, thud, down below, to which I had by now
become well accustomed.

There was a knock at my door, and Father McCarthy stepped in. "He's down below now," he said.

"Who?" I asked, very innocently.

"The ghost."

"No, Father," I replied very sweetly, "that's your imagination. It must be getting on your nerves." I could not resist that opportunity!

"Shall we go downstairs and investigate?" he asked.

"*We* shall go down if you like," I said, "but certainly I am not going alone."

So downstairs we went, and Father Mac called upon whoever or whatever it was to speak and make known what he or it wanted. No answer or sound of any kind, just a stilly and deathly silence which caused a chill up the spine.

The next morning at breakfast Father Keogh, not knowing anything of what happened, asked me if I had any experience the previous night. I proceeded to tell him.

"Go on," he said, "it all fits in with what I heard. Did you and Father McCarthy come up to bed together, or did one of you come up before the other?"

"We came up together, almost stair for stair!"

"Did you come up slowly or quickly?"

"Slowly."

"Then someone or something came running up the stairs some minutes before you, and went either into the bathroom or your bedroom."

"Thank you for telling me!"

So "the thing" which ran down the stairs heard by me alone, and created a disturbance heard by Father McCarthy and myself, passed us on his way up again heard only by Father Keogh.

Those are my two main experiences of the Plumstead *Poltergeist* though no doubt I had many minor ones which time has dimmed in my memory. Father McCarthy told me that "the thing" was very much quieter in my day than formerly, when so great was the noise and banging, that he expected to find all the furniture broken when he came down in the morning. As far as I can remember the servants were not troubled by it, and we did not speak about it to them.

I have called it the Plumstead *Poltergeist* because its manifestations were definitely of a *poltergeist* nature— quick heavy steps, banging and crashing about. But was it a *poltergeist*? We shall never know, but the sequel seems to indicate otherwise.

Father McCarthy had "inherited" from his predecessor a large cash box, which he had kept under his bed, but never opened. As an attempt was made to solve the ghostly problem he decided to investigate this box. It was solemnly brought down and opened in the presence of Father Keogh and myself, and the contents searched. Among other things we found a document appointing the former Rector as a trustee by a parishioner, to distribute weekly amounts to her husband from a sum of money which she proposed to leave for that purpose. There was also money left for, I think, twelve Masses, for the repose of her soul after her decease.

We looked back into the old Mass Registers and could find no evidence of the Masses ever having been said. In fact, by comparing dates, we came to the conclusion that the good priest had died before the parishioner. Perhaps he had accepted the money in advance, and so it happened that the Masses were never said. However that may have been, we agreed to say the Masses between us, and from then on the Presbytery has been left in peace. When Bishop Brown heard of that cash box incident he exclaimed: "No one will ever convince me that Dan McCarthy slept over a cash box for thirteen years without ever having looked into it! So that finished the Plumstead Ghost for me!"

It is clear from Father Loman's succinct memories that it was not a poltergeist but a perfectly justified appeal from a soul on the other side on behalf of claims to share in certain agreed Masses upon earth: a reason for manifestation which is not rare.

Part Two

CATHOLIC GHOST STORIES

I: INTRODUCTION

THE following collection is made within limitations. They are all stories of uncanny occurrences remembered in the Church. The old-fashioned type of story has slight attestation, and no attempt of evidence. It is only with recent stories that attempts are made to check and analyse.

The mediæval ghost story would yield a collection of itself. For instance, the sort of story that when Aix-la-Chapelle was built by Charlemagne and consecrated by Pope Leo III, two prelates failed to be present, but their absence did not detract from the splendour of the occasion, for two other prelates rose from the dead and took their places!

With the religious shiftings in England the old Catholic families kept apart from the national trend, were penalized and became self-centred and intermarried. They evolved types of the uncanny of their own.

It was a Lord Stourton (according to the Record Office) who wrote to Henry VIII's minion Cromwell about a vision attributed to the Prior of Hinton Charterhouse which appeared to forecast the execution of one of Henry's queens.

A famous story concerned the Elizabethan Lord Stourton, who had married the sister of the Stanley whose epitaph was written by Shakespeare. Under the pressure of the times he apostatized, but as a pious precaution he kept two priests, one as a day-chaplain and the other for night—just in case. He was stricken by a fit at the moment when neither was present. The night chaplain had gone off duty before his colleague had appeared. Lord Stourton summoned his wife and stated that he died a Catholic. The question then arose whether prayers could be said for Lord Stourton's soul. A priest, Father Cornelius, answered affirmatively and, when he was saying Mass for him the next day, Lord Stourton appeared on the Gospel side of the altar. Bishop Challoner in his *Memoirs of Missionary Priests* adds the name of the server who also saw His Lordship.

Archbishop David Mathew writing on the old Victorian Catholic society mentioned how,

> ...the conversation feathered round the ghost at Ince, where Charles Blundell was still reported to drag his lame leg on the stone-flagged passage. The ladies would aver that the ghosts were souls in Purgatory demanding Masses.

Old Catholic homes have never ceased to supply such stories mingled with hauntings. Lord Acton wrote in 1862 to Richard Simpson: "Has he got all the ghost stories from Acton Burnell?" (Seat of the Smythes in Shropshire.) I once followed Lord Acton's clue and learnt from Mrs. Ismay Bruce (*née* Smythe) that her,

> ...mother always laughed at Lord Acton's remark but she once heard of one. There were visitors at Acton Burnell and one morning a lady was woken by a maid who came in and said: "Mass is at 8 o'clock." Presently the ordinary maid with tea came in— but no one could ever account for the other maid.

It is only when scores of similar trivialities are collected that some pattern can be made out of the jig-saw

Slindon House in Sussex (an Eyre and Leslie seat and a Catholic oasis) was full of strange phenomena. Mrs. Violet Cogan (*née* Leslie) wrote (6th June 1937):

My old home Slindon House was most certainly haunted and the late Ernest Bowes-Lyon, who stayed with us many years ago, said: "Glamis is a joke compared to this house." Another place belonging to our family, Hassop Hall near Bakewell in Derbyshire, was also haunted.

Mrs. Mary Morse (*née* Leslie) told me she once saw the estate bricklayer at Slindon walking behind his two apprentices. This was odd because he had always preceded them. Odder still, it was the day after his funeral.

The ghost story for which Slindon was famous will be related later in the book.

Haunted presbyteries are common. St. Etheldreda's in Ely Place has always carried this supposition. Father O'Malley writes (2nd January 1950):

> Father Lockhart is said to have seen a lady with a lighted candle in her hand, going down the stairs of the Presbytery.
>
> A nun has been seen walking through the benches in the crypt towards the confessional box.
>
> Father Hickey, the late Provincial, is said to have seen a priest preceding him down the stairs at noon.
>
> Father Jarvis, a Rector here, told me some years ago that he had seen a lady in grey going through the blocked-in doorway connecting the two houses.

The annals of ghostdom can be very simple. Unclassified ghosts, unnamed phantoms appear at uncertain times. They have no story attached. But if one of these apparent discrepancies with the physical world, as we are taught to know it, can be proven true—then the attitude of Science and possibly of Religion must take a turn of the wheel, as though the compass could be shewn to point elsewhere than to the north *sometimes*.

Many convents are very happily and quietly haunted by the spirits of nuns who died in peace but are permitted to pay little visits or to finish up little tasks. Without giving any names, we can vouch for the following at first hand in an Order of nuns.

In one House, it was believed that a ghostly sister had been sometimes seen scrubbing the three steps outside the chapel. My informant told me that she never knew which steps they were until, as a girl going into the chapel, she noticed several times a sister scrubbing, but always passed her by. On one occasion she thought it was curious, because it was evening, and, turning round to look, she saw sister, bucket and all rise and dissolve in the air.

In the same House, on the occasion of the late Cardinal Hinsley's visit, two of the girls went down into the garden and, coming back, saw a nun they had never seen before. There was this remarkable fact that under her hood she wore a spotted veil.

In a country House of the same Order I was shewn a tree under which a deceased nun was seen by living sisters through a window.

Poets combine with scientists in record or research. So exquisite a nature as Gerard Manley Hopkins never failed to note stories practical or poetical. In his Diary of 1870 (p. 132), he notes a stained-glass window of the Blessed Virgin at Sion House which was annually broken and invisibly mended every year.

> A typical gleaning:
> Brother Slattery knew of a woman, who had buried three children, one unbaptized, at whose wake three lights or candles were seen in the yard, one weaker than the others. They were her children's souls come to accompany her. These candles seem to be the recognized form of apparition for departed souls.

But the whole of the literature belonging to the 'Celtic Twilight' belongs to another school of writing and classification.

II: FATHER JOHN GERARD'S GHOST-STORY

IN his Autobiography (translated from the Latin by Father Caraman, S.J.), the Elizabethan hero John Gerard, S.J., tells a story of a Holy Soul making sign from Purgatory (October 1591). A Catholic had died without a priest being brought to him, but expressing great desires to confess his sins.

These holy desires seem to have stood the dying man in good stead. Every night after his death his wife saw a kind of light flicker through the air in her room and enter past the bed-curtains. In her fright, she ordered her maidservants to bring their own beds into her room and stay with her during the night. But they saw nothing at all. Only the mistress saw it still every night and was very disturbed. In the end, she sent for her husband's Catholic friend, told him all that had happened and asked him to see some learned man to get his opinion. He in turn asked a priest who advised him to tell the lady that the strange light probably meant that she should come to the light of the faith. Her friend returned with this answer and she became a Catholic. After her reception, she had Mass said in that room for a long time. Yet the light still appeared every night. The widow was more worried than ever. The priest now consulted other priests. The answer they gave was this: probably her husband was on his way to heaven (he had been a Catholic at heart and had wanted to receive the sacraments) but he still needed prayers for the purgation of his soul. He suggested, therefore, that Mass should be offered for him for thirty days according to the old custom of the country. The lady arranged for this, and went to Communion herself several times with the same intention. The night after the last Mass had been offered in the room, three lights appeared instead of the customary one, the outside two seeming to support the third between them. All three entered past the bed-curtains, and after staying a few moments they mounted heavenwards through the top coverings, leaving her in great comfort of soul. Nothing of the kind appeared again, and she interpreted it all as a sign that her husband's soul had been freed from suffering and carried up by the angels to heaven. This happened in the County of Stafford.

III: THE APPARITION OF A NUN

MOTHER BENEDICTA SOMERS was head of the Loreto Convent at Gorey in Wexford during the 'fifties, when the Oxford Movement was producing echoes in Ireland. This holy nun set out to pray for the conversion of the local landlord, Mr. Ram, and family. Mrs. Ram was in Paris at the time that Mother Benedicta was dying. She wrote afterwards to Fr. Francis Kirk of the Oblates of St Charles in Bayswater:

> I was not well, and went to bed early. I felt no inclination to sleep. After a short time the door seemed to open, and, to my great surprise, I saw the Rev. Mother of Gorey enter my room. I was not alarmed, only surprised. She said nothing, but beckoned to me to leave my bed and follow her. It seemed to me that I actually did leave the bed and followed her into a large room. Though I was in my own house I had never seen that room before ... there I beheld a huge Cross, without any figure, emitting dazzling rays. I stood in rapture before it. A slight touch from the Rev. Mother recalled me to myself. She then spoke these words in a soft voice:
>
> "My child, it is of no use to stand admiring the beauties of the Cross: it will not benefit you unless you embrace and carry it. Pray for strength to do that which you know to be right." These last words were repeated two or three times.

The Parish Priest of Gorey, Father Lacy, may take up the story:

> All the nuns were praying about her bedside, waiting for her last moment. Suddenly, to our great astonishment, she who had been utterly unable to move sat up in her bed, and with a loud voice spoke these words: "I have been praying for years for the

conversion of this family. Now I am on the point of appearing before Almighty God, and I offer my life for their conversion." Immediately after the words were spoken she fell back and expired.

IV: A PRIEST RETURNING ON ACCOUNT OF MASSES UNSAID

A COMMON type of ghost in Catholic circles is the return of the spirit of some priest anxious that Masses should be said for himself or on the score of Masses left unsaid. To such spirits the abiding memory is of the Mass which they offered daily for the living and the dead. As the great bond between spirits upon earth and spirits in Purgatory, its omission would be liable to bring about what is here described.

I owe the following to Father Bernard Kelly of Brixton. It corroborates the Plumstead poltergeist with slight discrepancy:

> After the death of the Rector of St Patrick's, Plumstead, the Rev. Arthur Staunton, in 1913, the clergy there were troubled every night for a long while by noises in the Presbytery, in fact for about a year and a half. The new Rector, Rev. Daniel McCarthy, now Canon, had the feeling that it was this good priest who wanted something to be done that he had left undone.
>
> "Whenever I went for a holiday," the Canon informs me, "all was quiet but when I returned, he was back again!" So the Canon proceeded to investigate and he came across a will by some old lady living in the parish, directing that after her death Father Staunton was to say ten Masses for her and her husband. It was discovered that the old lady had died in St Bartholomew's Hospital eighteen months before, which corresponded with the time the noises were first heard in the Presbytery, so the Masses were at once said and the noises ceased.
>
> The ghost came back again on the following Christmas night and it was an expression of joy and thankfulness. The omission of the Masses was not through Father Staunton's fault as he was an

invalid for a year before he died and had in fact survived the Testatrix by several months.

V: A PRIEST INSISTING ON HIS RIGHTS

ONE of the strangest stories that I ever heard came from the lips of a bishop, the late Dr. Lyons of Kilmore, who referred me to the Bishop of Galway. He had heard it at the same time when the story was told at Maynooth in 1935 by the priest who brought the Irish setter dog mentioned into the American mission field, the scene of the story. The tale ran:

An Irish priest received his first appointment as pastor in a small parish some distance from civilization. His predecessor was an old Irish priest, Father D——.[3] He had not died there, but had been taken to a hospital. Through some mistake on the part of the diocesan office, his successor, Father O'F——, was appointed as pastor, not as administrator. As apparently the man was still alive, they took it that it would be only a matter of a short time until he died. The old man lived for some time after the other was appointed to his parish. He seems to have been insistent on his rights as Parish Priest, as he expressed a definite desire that on his death his remains should be brought back to his parish church, left there for one night, and then brought back to some church in the city where his funeral could be more conveniently attended by the clergy. The old man died, and his wishes were not carried out. Through some oversight, or because it was too much trouble, his remains were not brought to the church for the customary night before the altar. Hence, not merely had he been deprived of his right and title as P.P. by the precipitate appointment of a successor, but he had been denied the traditional favour of resting before the altar where he had been P.P.

---

[3] The names of the priests are kept anonymous.

81

His successor had made several visits to Ireland since his appointment. On returning after his last visit he brought back with him a magnificent red setter dog. Shortly after his predecessor died, the dog began to make himself a nuisance by howling in a most disturbing manner at night. Every night he kept up this mournful howling, to the great surprise of the P.P., who, however, was a man of very sound nerves. Then, on the Saturday after his annual retreat, he came back to his parish from the city, heard confessions, locked the front door of the church, put out the main switch, and, previous to leaving through the sacristy, knelt for a few moments in the dark before the high altar. Suddenly the lights went on, the front door opened, and he heard the click as the leaves of the door swung back into their catches. He looked around and saw a coffin coming up the middle passage supported on nothing, but about two or three feet from the ground. He fled through the sacristy to his house, which stood beside the church. As he rushed through the front room of the house he glanced out through the window at the church; the lights were out. In the morning, there was no sign of the doors having been opened.

Some days passed, and nothing happened, but the setter kept up the howling. Then one morning, after early Mass, he was kneeling in the church, making his thanksgiving. He had to say Mass early, as the few who attended it had to get early into the city. He was alone in the church; it was a fine, warm morning in July. Suddenly he heard the doors of the church swing open and the lights went on: he looked back, and there again he saw the coffin coming up the central passage. This time he felt no panic. The coffin stood supported on air in front of the altar. He got up from his knees, went to the sacristy, put on soutane, surplice and stole, took his ritual and the holy water, came out and stood before the altar. He read the prayers which are said for the Absolution when a body is removed from the church for burial. Then he walked round the coffin sprinkling it with holy water. As he did so, he noticed that the head of the coffin was towards the altar, according to the canonical custom, in the case of a priest, and that the name on the breastplate was that of his predecessor. He finished the prayers calmly and walked back to the sacristy. The coffin withdrew, and he heard the doors closing. That night the setter did not howl or any night after.

This story is not without confirmation. By pure chance I met the brother of Fr. O'F—— in England. His addition, whether it preceded or followed what has been given, was that his brother's red setter showed alarm and bristled. He looked up and saw his church was lit up. He entered and saw Father D—— enter to say Mass and ask for a server. Next day Fr O'F—— rushed round to inform his Archbishop of the whole story. The Archbishop said, "Poor Father John," and they agreed to say his Masses for him, presuming that some had been left unsaid.

VI: GODFREY RAUPERT'S WARNING

IT is agreed that psychical research can be dangerous. Evil spirits may lead to obsession. Religious belief and moral character may be damaged. As an object lesson Father Thurston prescribed a story from J. Godfrey Raupert, a convert Anglican clergyman, who used to lecture in seminaries on the dangers that Spiritualism could produce:

> I was being entertained as a guest by H. E. Cardinal Vaughan. He had very kindly invited me to spend a fortnight with him at Archbishop's House to prepare for my reception into the Catholic Church. English Society was taking a lively interest in Spiritualism at that time and conversations on this at table in Archbishop's House were of daily occurrence. The Cardinal often spoke of the deep concern he felt about the growth of this new craze and he seemed bent on finding means to counteract the movement and to put the curious on their guard. I noticed His Eminence's private secretary was unusually well informed about Spiritualism. Soon after my reception the Cardinal called upon me to lecture on Spiritualism. He also invited the clergy of the Archdiocese to a lecture and presided himself. If I am not mistaken, this was his last public appearance before his death (1903).
>
> About two years later I found myself at an evening party in London at which a lady was discussing Spiritualism and happened to mention that in the séance she was describing a Catholic priest had taken part. I ventured to express a doubt. The lady however to my astonishment mentioned the name of the priest, a young Monsignor, the Cardinal's secretary.

The death of the Cardinal had, it seems, released this young man from his secretarial duties. I paid him a visit and asked him to tell me his experiences. It was palpable that this new interest had made a deep impression on him. What had occurred he recounted as follows.

The Medium had readily submitted to all the conditions required of him. The host, a distinguished General, had so stiffened these conditions that the company were fully satisfied. The séance was held in a locked room and in semi-darkness.

To the boundless astonishment of the young ecclesiastic there came forward from behind the curtain a materialized figure. Stature and features were those of the deceased Cardinal. It came straight to him and whispered into his ear: "What I taught during my earth life is not the truth. I found this out as soon as I came to the world in which I now live. Tell everybody that you have spoken with me and make known what I have said. ..."

After long hesitation, he made up his mind to have recourse to an elderly prelate [Mgr. Moyes] and asked his counsel. The prelate believed there was trickery on the part of the spirits and that the phantom could not be really the late Cardinal. He drew up a list of questions to be put to the phantom hoping that the imposture would be made manifest. I only know that they were answered more or less satisfactorily. For another test, certain objects were obtained. One of these was the little red cap which Cardinal Vaughan had worn. This the Monsignor slipped into the breast pocket of his coat. The phantom, so he informed me, appeared as usual, walked straight up to him and said, "I see that you have something in your pocket which belongs to me." Thereupon he took the cap out of the pocket and set it upon his own head. After the figure dematerialized, the cap was found upon the carpet.

The matter now took on a very serious aspect. It seemed absolutely necessary to carry the investigation further. After long debates, another question was drawn up which turned on an affair with which only three people were acquainted: the dead Cardinal, the young Monsignor, and the Duke of Norfolk. As the project debated between them had not been carried out, the matter had never come to the knowledge of the public. The questions to be asked dealt with the particular obstacles which in the opinion of the three had rendered it inadvisable to proceed further.

The phantom, so the Monsignor assured me, answered all the questions so exactly that no doubt was left in his mind that he was holding converse with the dead Cardinal himself. This conviction was attended with a complete loss of faith in the Catholic Church. He gave up his life as a priest and became an ardent Spiritualist. All the attempts I made by narrating my own experiences, to recall him from this desperate course, proved unavailing. ...

In any case the disillusionment I had predicted did not fail to come about. He wrote me a very touching letter which I treasure as a document of lasting value. What he said was:

"I have carefully read your book [*The Supreme Problem*] and I am convinced it will do a great deal of good. I know that the clergy think more of the work of a layman than of the treatises of theologians which often pass unheeded. ... So far as regards myself I have definitely made up my mind and nothing in the world will induce me to have anything more to do with Spiritualism. It was a long time before I came to this conclusion and I hope that it may still be possible for me to retrace my steps, but we only find out the strength of the current when we attempt to battle against it in order to reach the shore."

This was Raupert's story and I have condensed the copy in Father Thurston's handwriting. Raupert added that the ex-Monsignor was now attending Mass as a layman and regular communicant. So all was well that ended well.[4]

The Hon. Everard Feilding, who had travelled some of these dangerous latitudes without losing his Catholic Faith in the least, alluded to this Monsignor in a letter (9th February 1935).

You ask if I met Mgr. ——. Yes, many years ago I went several times to sittings with Husk at Gamber Bolton's studio, and Mgr. —— was also there. I think he came to see me in John Street. I lost sight of him and have no notion of what became of him. I vaguely think someone told me he had ceased to be a priest. The sittings did not convince me in the least though the phenomena were very effective. The trouble was that the sitters were such utter geese.

---

[4] It may be added that the chief actor in his return was Abbot Marmion "who made the mystical substitution of 'life for soul' and after packing him off to Heaven, caught some skin-complaint that took a lot of curing." (Information from Mgr. Barton.)

Feilding's sceptical opinion was carefully reasoned but Raupert was certainly convinced. One can only attribute such a materialization to brilliant conjuring (of the Maskelyne and Cook variety) or possibly to a clever demon armed with thought-reading powers. The secret shared between the Monsignor, Cardinal Vaughan, and the Duke of Norfolk appears to have been the exact method of enshrining the relics of a supposed St. Edmund in Westminster Cathedral. Serious obstacles arose to the whole idea, as recounted in *Cardinal Vaughan's Life* by Snead-Cox, but certain details of the final treatment of the relics, had they proved genuine, remained a secret with very few.

VII: EVERARD FEILDING'S CASE OF A BLEEDING PICTURE

A CASE that had profoundly interested the Hon. Everard Feilding he communicated to Cardinal Gasquet. It concerned a bleeding picture of the Holy Face and bleeding Hosts, caused by a highly mediumized priest in the Poitiers diocese.

Feilding wrote to Cardinal Gasquet from Caire (21st February 1917).

My DEAR EMINENCE,

You will be surprised to get a letter from me out of the blue and probably snigger when you hear the object of it. You may have heard of my dabblings in spooks and such things. If not, I must break it to you that I do dabble in them experimentally as Hon. Sec. of the Society for Psychical Research in succession (a long way after) to Frederic Myers. And I am troubling you in order to ask, if you will tell me, if you know anything of the strange case of the Abbé Vachèn de Gratteloup of Mirebeau en Poitou, excommunicated in about June 1914 for having miracles *chez lui*. I had heard of the case in 1913 and finding myself in Paris in May 1914 went down to Mirebeau and introduced myself to the Abbé and heard his story as follows. In 1905 a pious female gave him a cheap oleograph of the Sacred Heart which he pinned up over his altar in his private chapel. In Oct. 1911, while saying Mass, he noticed some dark stains on the forehead of this picture. Examining it after Mass he found they looked like blood-stains. A few days after, 'there were more, and later more still. He began taking a series of photos, about 20 in number, which he showed me; and in which you can follow the gradual developments; first, a few dark marks on the forehead, then one mark forms into a drop

88

and runs down, then another, then marks show on the hands, then on the heart, then more run down and so on, till, at the end of the series, the picture is covered with blood-streams from brow, hands and heart and a regular "crown of thorns" of clotted blood is formed on the brow, like a Carlo Dolce *Ecco Homo*. Of course, it became a local wonder and crowds came to see. The Bishop of Poitiers, Humbrecht, a Franco-Alsatian of, from description, indifferent spirituality but decided views cried "Fraud," and told him to stop it. The Abbé replied that, if the picture insisted on bleeding, it wasn't his fault, and there were unpleasant passages. Eventually the Bishop ordered him to send him the picture, which eventually and under protest, he did. And he pinned up another one; not in his chapel but in a cottage a kilometre away. The next day, he was informed by a workman who lived there that this picture had also begun to bleed. "Rats," said the Abbé (more or less) and paid no attention. The following day the workman again returned and insisted that it was going on and the Abbé went up to see. And then precisely the same sequel took place with this second picture. I asked the Abbé whether it was bleeding then. He said he didn't know; that it bled in cycles of a few days at a time, then stopped for a few days, and then began again, and that he hadn't been to see for a little time. We accordingly went up to the hill on which the cottage, now empty, stood, unlocked the door, and there, sure enough, was the picture covered with streams of what looked like fresh wet blood, i.e., long marks with drops at the bottom of them consisting of a serum-like fluid, and many stains on the floor and on the few artificial daisies standing below. So much for the picture. On the way, he explained that this by no means exhausted his miracle, but that on many occasions the "miracle of Bolsena" of the Raphael stanze had been repeated at his Mass; i.e., that the consecrated Host had bled. He had kept several of the Hosts, and on returning to his house, opened his tabernacle and showed me two or three lunettes containing Hosts covered with what appeared to be deep-red bloodstains. A few months before my visit, he said, he had just come to the Elevation, and raised the Host, when a large drop of blood fell from it. Much shaken, he put it down on the Corporal, and started a new Mass with another Host. When he had finished, he found that the Host had bled so copiously that it had soaked through the Corporal to the altar cloth, and got stuck. So he decided to leave it there, put some battens of wood on each side, covered the whole up with another cloth and shifted henceforth, for Mass purposes, to another alter. He removed the cloths and showed me the Host, lying about two feet from the edge of the altar. From it there came a thick stream of dried blood as far as the edge. This he said had gradually formed owing to successive bleedings at intervals of several weeks until the stream reached the edge and flowed over so that he had to put cloths below to catch it. Well, that finishes my visit of 1914, excepting, and this in the light of events is interesting—that he said he constantly heard a voice prophesying immediate and awful things for France, and hearing that Maud Gonne, who with W. B. Yeats had accompanied me, lived in Paris, he begged her to come at once.

In May 1916, having a few days' leave from my work at the Admiralty, I went unexpectedly over to Mirebeau, without announcing myself. I found the Abbé saying his rosary in his garden. He wasn't at all pleased to see me, told me he had been excommunicated, and was much harried by the clerical party and even denounced as a German spy and had had three police perquisitions who came to hunt for wireless in his Calvary and gun-replacements etc. and that he had had to move the picture down again to his own chapel. I immediately went in to see it, and found it again covered with much blood. Having brought microscope slides and medicated blotting paper, I took a number of samples and completely dried the picture up. Next morning it was again all wet. I again dried it, locked the chapel door and took the key away. In the evening, I returned and again found the picture wet as before. Whether there was a duplicate key I cannot say. If not, nobody could have got in, for the windows were tiny and high up. Next morning the picture was again wet, and I dried it, and this time stayed all day either in the chapel or close by. The picture did not get wet. Towards evening the Abbé came to inspect. He said it was regrettable that it wouldn't bleed when it was wanted to, but that it was very irregular in its habits. He said he believed the blood formed *under* the big blood scabs which cover the picture and that only when there is enough does it come out. He pressed with his finger on one of them, and a little fluid exuded. As for the Host on the altar, that was still there, but since my visit of the year 1914, had thrown forth two more blood streams, each reaching the edge.

On returning to London I had my samples analysed at the Lister Institute. They were too busy with war-research work to carry the analysis up to the last stage, which determines whether it is *human* blood as apart from animal blood, but they said there was no doubt of its being, at all events, *mammalian* blood.

Enquiry a few months ago eliciting that the picture was now bleeding more than ever, I wrote to a very clever, highly educated French lady friend, and suggested her going down to Mirebeau to see. She went about Christmas time 1916, presenting herself, as a stranger and not mentioning my name. On her way, she called on the Bishop of Poitiers to get his side of the story. He received her graciously, but with *la grâce d'un ours*[5]; first denied that anything happened at all; but eventually admitted that the picture did bleed real blood, but that it must be a fraud because the Abbé was so rebellious about it, as well as on *a priori* grounds. Bishops, like the Psychical Society, the existence of both of whom depends on the assumption of the *possibility* of the supernatural, or at least supernormal, have a tendency at once to say "fraud" when they come across an alleged concrete example of it. But he had never been to Mirebeau to see it himself, nor I think had even had any examination made whatever. Altogether, an unenterprising common-sense Bishop, who, as the Abbé tells me, condemns the Boy Scouts in his diocese. My friend went on to see the Abbé and writes me a long, highly entertaining and decidedly favourable report of her impressions. The picture was still bleeding. Now there's my case. Not final, I grant you, because until one can establish that the picture absolutely bleeds without possibility of access, there is no case at all, except a very strange study in human psychology. Because, if the Abbé is performing all this mystification *deliberately*, it is one of the queerest cases of religious criminality, or, *if not deliberately*, of criminal lunacy I have ever heard of. The Abbé was well known in Rome some years ago, and after my visit I wrote to ask Cardinal Merry about him, as he knew him well. He answered, rather shortly, that he [knew] nothing of the reasons of the condemnation or of whether there was any evidence of fraud, but that he had always thought the Abbé *exalté* and a little dotty. That is hardly the impression any of us got of him. He seems a pious old gentleman, very full of his miracle of course, rather oppressed by it; very cross with the Bishop who condemns him without the least enquiry; very cross with the Vatican which excommunicates him without any trial at all; rather humorous; charitable; respected in the town, as far as I could understand by talking at the inn; lives very quietly; sees hardly anybody; doctors the poor with herbs, for which he has a reputation; well-educated and artistic in a Franco-ecclesiastical

---

[5] "the grace of a bear" – i.e. grouchy.

kind of way, with some good pictures by other artists and pictures by himself; embroiders, gardens and so on. My friend is going for a more extended examination at Easter and perhaps I shall be able to supplement this, if it at all interests you. Meanwhile, the old gentleman clamours to be investigated by competent authority, and surely, as a strange incident in ecclesiastical history it merits a proper enquiry. He admits that he writes rude letters to the Pope, but then so would your Eminence, if you had a picture that *would* bleed and you were denounced for it by a Bishop who forbade Boy Scouts. My reason in writing all this screed is to ask whether, if the case interests you sufficiently to make enquiry as to the evidence before the excommunicating authorities, you will do so and let me know what there is in it.

The Abbé's case is that it was a warning of the War, an exhortation to France to turn from iniquities and a divine, if somewhat crude, exhibition of the interest felt in Heaven in her condition. Well perhaps. But, anyhow, isn't it queer?

(25th March 1917).

I have just received your letter. I am grateful to you for not turning down my own; for I am convinced that whatever conclusion one may ultimately come to regarding this strange story, i.e., whether it is a "miracle," divine or diabolic, or merely a fraud, it has a serious interest in the subject of the making of religions, and is worth coming to the bottom of, if possible, by some more satisfactory method than a mere ecclesiastical combination. I wrote last week to the Abbé, telling him I had written to you and asking him to send you some photos of the picture taken at such intervals as will show the developments of the "phenomenon."

I have also received a further explanatory letter from my French friend with regard to one or two points which were not clear in her first account. You will remember that in my letter to you I had said that although the picture, after being dried up, had bled afresh in my absence, it had not done so in my presence. I had asked my friend specially to ascertain whether there was evidence that this had taken place with any reliable person. She answered that she had herself seen a linen cloth gradually covered with blood. I wrote to ask for details, and she answers: "*L'abbé V. de G. avait placé sous mon contrôle un linge blanc, au pied de l'image et devant moi le sang ne cessa de couler assez rapidement pour couvrir ou imbiber peu à peu le linge tout entiel' dans l'espace d'une heure environ.*"[6] This description lacks particularity, I admit, but you must remember that the picture only consists of a medium-sized oleograph in a plain wooden frame, unglazed and unbacked, so that one can see the plain paper, scarcely discoloured, at the back. She adds: "*j'avoue que je ne vois pas comment avait pu être produite ainsi sous mes yeux une supercherie quelconque.*"[7] As for the Bishop's attitude to which you very naturally attach importance, she says that he "*admet le fait, mais l'explique par le pouvoir de Lucifer se jouant de lois scientifiques que nous ne connaîtrions pas encore.*"[8] This is typically bishopesque (saving your presence!) and doesn't carry us further. I think the origin of his attitude is that he was angry at the Abbé at first declining to give the picture up to him, and felt that a man who could flout a Bishop must *obviously* be possessed by the devil. Perhaps he is, but, after all the works of the devil are only second in interest (and often superior in entertainment) to those of Anybody Else. Unless the Abbé lies heroically, and in a way that could easily be found out, the Bishop had certainly not conducted any real enquiry, except possibly by examining the picture when it was eventually sent to him. My friend further says that the Abbé has written to her to say that the picture (i.e., the new one which took, the place of the original one sent to the Bishop) has for the moment stopped manifesting, but that on the other hand the Host on the altar had again begun "*à émettre des flots de sang qui foulent jusque sur les marches, par terre.*"[9] ... Did I tell you that the Abbé declares that the Voice tells him that the picture is to be carried along the Front, and that until that is done, this carnage will continue? It is the moral unreason of such a statement as that that specially upsets one and that lends a confirmation to Cardinal Merry's statement that the Abbé was slightly dotty, and unsound. But when all is so strange, it is difficult to distinguish one element of dottiness from another, and anyway, I much hope

---

[6] "The Abbe V. de G. had placed under my control a white cloth at the foot of the image, and before me the blood never ceased to flow quickly enough to cover or gradually soak the whole linen for the space of about an hour."

[7] "I confess that I do not see how such a deception could have been produced before my eyes."

[8] "Admits the fact, but explains it by the power of Lucifer playing with scientific laws that we do not know yet."

[9] "To emit streams of blood which were trampled on the steps, on the ground."

that you will be able to help at arriving at some more satisfactory conclusion than that of the Bishop.

The Cardinal's letters are not extant.
Many years later I made inquiries in the Bishopric of Poitiers and received brief word from the Vicar General 16th January 1950):

Cher confrère, Le prêtre dont vous parlez a été excommunié. Agréez, cher confrère, mes respectueuses salutations.[10]

So that is that.
To the author Everard Feilding wrote (12th April 1922) concerning Spiritualism:

> The more I see of that subject the less do I know where I stand, either intellectually or sympathetically, regarding it. The folly of its propagandists revolts me. Once I read a paper to the Newman Society at Oxford to an audience largely composed of Jesuits. My text was that psychical research should be encouraged by the Church as a useful branch of ecclesiastical activity. I pointed out that the great difficulty of most people was to accept the one inevitable foundation of all interest in a personal religious system, a conviction viz. of continuance of consciousness after death, and that if this could, by psychical research methods, be shewn to be so extremely probable that it became a matter of knowledge of the same class as, say, the rings of Saturn, certain in existence and only doubtful in quality, religious teachers would be saved a world of trouble. The Jesuits would have none of me. They thought it wouldn't help at all. This seemed and still seems to me very odd.

The suggestion might be put in this manner: that if psychical research makes the web visible or comprehensible, Religion completes the tapestry by revealing the weft. Some inquiries could never achieve one

---

[10] "Dear colleague, The priest of whom you speak was excommunicated. Accept, dear colleague, my respectful greetings."

without the other.

VIII: CARDINAL GASQUET
RECORDS A GHOST

WHEN Cardinal Manning started work in Bayswater, he introduced the Oblates of St. Charles. Amongst his followers during the Fifties were the Gasquet family and Father Laprimadaye, who had been his curate in Anglican days at Lavington.

More than half a century later Francis Gasquet had become a Cardinal and in his reminiscences recorded how his sisters saw the ghost of Father Laprimadaye.

> When the Oblates moved from 12 Sutherland Place into their permanent home, my mother took the lease of their old house and here a curious incident happened, which may be recorded. Amongst the Oblates who had been living in the house was Father Laprimadaye. He had a small room at the top of the house, and my sisters had the top floor when we went to live there. One night, my mother being away, my sisters on going upstairs to bed, saw a figure, which they thought resembled Father Laprimadaye, passing into the room he had before occupied. My brother and I, who were on the floor below, heard the cries they uttered and going up found the reason. We noted the time, and next morning we told the Oblate Fathers what had happened, and we all concluded that it was one of those cases where the wraith of someone on the hour of death is allowed to visit a place where he had been. We afterwards found that Father Laprimadaye had died in Rome at the time.

A future Cardinal was connected with a famous ghost story told in Lady Bloomfield's *Reminiscences* (Vol. II, p. 266), where Princess Schönberg described how her mother

Princess Pauline Schwarzenberg, was burnt in a fire at the Austrian Embassy in Paris.

> She had left her youngest children here at Vienna. The Cardinal being then a baby of six months old was in his cradle one night, when his nurse, an old and very respectable but by no means clever or imaginative woman, suddenly fell down on her knees and exclaimed: "Jesu, Joseph, Maria! There is the figure of the Princess standing over the baby's cradle!" Several nursery maids who were in the room heard the exclamation though they saw nothing: but to her dying day the nurse affirmed the truth of the vision, and there being then no telegraph, it was not for many days after that the news of the Princess Schwarzenberg's untimely fate reached Vienna.

Once again the spirit of the just was allowed to visit a place dear to the soul at the hour of death.

IX: A PRIEST'S COLLECTION

FATHER BERNARD KELLY wrote to me from Corpus Christi House, Brixton (22nd October 1945): "Herewith I send you my eerie *omnium gatherum* of alleged hauntings, a rather mixed lot."

1. The Bermondsey Ghost

THE Catholic Church of the Most Holy Trinity, Bermondsey, which grew out of an old "Mass House" founded close to East Lane in 1773 largely through the efforts of the Rev. Gerard Shaw, a friend of Bishop Challoner (died 1781), became the centre of a reported haunting in the early nineties of last century. An "old-fashioned looking" priest was reported to have been seen occasionally in the Presbytery, sometimes on the stairs, and now and then in one of the rooms. My old friend the late Rev. Joseph Haynes (died 1925), the Rector of the Catholic Church, Paradise Street, Rotherhithe, informed me that he believed he saw the ghost when calling at the Bermondsey Presbytery one morning in the summer of about 1894. He was waiting in the room of Father (later Canon) Edward Murnane the Rector and meanwhile reading a current copy of the *Daily Telegraph*. Looking up he saw an old priest standing near the window. He spoke to the priest twice but getting no reply concluded that he was deaf and so went on reading. He looked up again and saw the priest a second time, but when preparing to leave, as he could wait no longer, found the priest had gone. This much surprised

Father Haynes as he had not heard any footsteps or even the door close. However, just then Father Murnane came in and after referring to the object of his call Father Haynes remarked:

"Who is that old priest I saw here a few minutes ago?"

"Old priest," replied Father Murnane. "We have no old priest here!"

"Oh yes," stressed Father Haynes, "it was certainly an old priest I distinctly saw in this room just now."

Then Father Murnane said: "Well, I suppose it must have been the ghost that haunts this place. He has been seen more than once."

As a result of this incident, the priests at Holy Trinity and some of the neighbouring churches said Mass for the supposed "intentions" of the *Revenant* and no more reappearances occurred. Judged by his appearance the ghostly priest seemed to be of the late 18th century and it may have been the spirit of the priest who served the Bermondsey Mission about 1780-1800, and who left a number of Mass "intentions" unsaid. But of course, this is mere conjecture. I may add that Father Baynes, who died in April 1925, was a very matter of fact man, one not at all interested in psychical topics but on the contrary rather inclined to regard cases of alleged hauntings as mere instances of a vivid imagination!

2. The Southwark Ghosts

THE late Rev. Frederick Wilderspin, a very esteemed priest of the Diocese of Southwark and sometime Religious Examiner of its Schools, told me an interesting story about his friend the Rev. Roderick Moore, with whom he was associated when at St. George's Cathedral, Southwark. Father Moore had studied for the priesthood after the death of his wife and was ordained about 1890. Much of the few years of his sacerdotal life was spent on the staff of the

Cathedral. Shortly after his death in 1893 his friend Father Wilderspin was in his room at St. George's when suddenly he saw Father Moore standing near the window. Surprised, of course, but not alarmed, Father Wilderspin took what steps he could to make sure that the apparition was no mere imagination and, as many other Catholics no doubt would conclude in like circumstances, he considered that probably his friend was in Purgatory and wanted prayers. Several Masses were subsequently offered for the repose of the soul of the deceased priest and there was never any repetition of what appears to have been a reminder for pious suffrages from the other world.

3. Return of a Canon

CANON DOYLE, who did so much towards the foundation of St. George's Cathedral, has also been raised to the uncanny dignity of a *Revenant*! The late Mr. William Bird, so long the very efficient sacristan, told me that several elderly members of the congregation, persons of education and judgment, had more than once declared that they had seen the Canon in the Cathedral years after his death, which occurred in the summer of 1879. One reason given for this startling occurrence was an alleged declaration of the Canon that he would "turn in his grave" if the fine sanctuary screen by Pugin, the architect of the Cathedral, were ever removed from its original position! The screen was transferred to near the entrance of the Cathedral and it was apparently after this time that the Canon made his return to earth to protest presumably against what he, no doubt, regarded as an act of vandalism!

X: GUARDIAN ANGEL IN PICCADILLY

THE following is taken from *Father Steuart, S.J.: A Study of his Life and Teaching* by Katharine Kendall:

Two curious incidents are recorded of this time. One night he went up to London, got into a hansom and gave an address to the driver. He was off to some rendezvous to meet another young dare-devil who had an influence on him which was not of the best. In Piccadilly, the hansom was held up in a traffic jam. A young man he had never seen before stepped on to it and said three words: "Don't go there." Then he disappeared. But Robert was so deeply impressed that he reversed his order to the driver. It is not every day that one meets one's Guardian Angel in Piccadilly.

Another time it was after some celebration which had been fast and furious and Bobby, it is regretfully recorded, was blind to the world. He was brought back to the hotel where the family always stayed, and the proprietor, who reported the incident, said that a most beautiful young man carried him in and put him down on a chair in the hall. A most beautiful young man, he repeated again and again, and he went away without a word. The culprit, needless to say, knew nothing at all about it but his family always believed that his Guardian Angel had come to the rescue once more.

XI: THEY DO NOT DIE!

THE late Mr. James Durham of Raynham allowed me to use this brief account of his only son's survival after death in battle.

> In 1942—early 1943 Nicholas was in Hospital in Durban and there met and apparently made great friends with Geoffrey Hutchison. He was a New Zealander and had a Commission at Durban, now living at Pietermaritzberg.
>
> He and Mrs. Laurence Humphries of Claremont, near Capetown, told my son's wife the following story:
>
> He saw Nicholas at 8 o'clock standing by a high wall, in uniform and shorts and spoke to him— "Are you alive?" And Nicholas answered, "No. Geoffrey, I am afraid I am not."
>
> This apparition of my dearly loved son occurred in August 1943. I was not told it until years later. Last year I wrote to Mr. Humphries again and my letter was returned—"not sufficiently addressed."

With two devastating wars the veil has worn thin and it must be getting thinner with the vast weight of sighs coming from this side and the immense desire to hold out hands across seas infinite and eternal. Mourners in their agony can place themselves into touch with the dead and, if God permits—obtain manifestation or sign from the other side. Maybe it is only a natural flower which, placed before a photograph or a shrine, refuses to wither—perhaps only a picture that falls or a waking dream in which voice and vision come in a split second of time to the awakened. The apparition of those who were snatched away too soon must still obey that secret ordinance of God which St.

Augustine once conjectured.

XII: A BENEDICTINE RECOVERS THE DATE OF A MARTYRDOM IN A DREAM

THE late Abbot Ethelbert Home, a Benedictine of Downside Abbey, put this paper in my hands before his death in 1953.

On January 23, 1888, just before the "call up" for Matins, I had the following dream. I thought that Dom Meurad Fulton stood by my bedside with a skull in his hand, the back of it turned towards me. Across the skull on the lower part of the back, were several lines of bad scrawly writing, beginning much higher up on the left hand side, and running downwards to the right. On the last line I saw distinctly the date.

8 March 1607

...then a little more writing and then a D followed by some letters smudged out. I said to Dam Meurad, "What a pity, I cannot read just the part I want," meaning what followed the D, as it was evidently the name of the owner of the skull. I then tried to take the head from him; but between us we dropped it on the floor. The noise made by the fall was that of the "call up" knocking at my door, which woke me and put an end to the dream. Immediately on getting up, I looked at Challoner's Missionary Priests for 1607 and found Fr. Rob. Drury, but read the date March 24th. When I found the dates did not agree, I treated the whole thing as a dream, and thought no more of it. During the day, I mentioned the matter to two or three others, and the next day Dom Gilbert Dolan told me my date was correct, as Fr. Drury suffered on February 26th, 1607, and with the difference for old and new style, this makes the date I saw, namely March 8th. Dom Meurad says he knows nothing of the affair!

The writing on the skull was somewhat like the sketch, but I cannot remember if the 8 was before the word March, or after it. The space between the figures of the year, was as I have drawn it.

ETHELBERT HORNE, O.S.B.

January 25, 1888.

The drawing shows four lines of writing with the date thus: 8 March 16 0 7—D

XIII: THE GHOST WHO TURNED THE DOOR HANDLE

IN his Reminiscences Professor Sayce, the great Oxford Orientalist, describes how he attended the Oriental Congress in Florence in 1890 accompanied by Mr. Seager, who had once been Pusey's assistant but had become a Catholic. He had professed Hebrew at Cardinal Manning's College in South Kensington. He died in Florence during the Congress apparently of old age. Sayce continues:

The night of Seager's death the three of us were again together in Bywater's room; Seager's body was already lying in its coffin not far away and our conversation naturally turned upon sudden death. By degrees we passed to other subjects and it was growing dark when we all three simultaneously heard the handle of the door turned and furthermore saw it turning. As the door did not open, Stillman rose and opened it himself. No one was to be seen from one end of the corridor to the other. The occurrence made a great impression upon him; more than once in after years he reverted to it saying, "The hand that tried to turn the handle was like that of a feeble old man." Seager died in Catholic Grace but may have wished to make a farewell to his colleagues.

XIV : THE MASS-ECHO IN TIME

THERE is a widespread story which I have been anxious to collect but I have found elusive. It is the story of the remains of pre-Reformation altars or wooden furniture used for Mass in Penal times. Whether stone or wooden, these remains had the power of making music heard by children, probably of the type to whom fairies materialize. This music is accompanied by chants in an unknown language. They turn out to be plain-chant and Latin, reminiscent of the old Catholic services. In November 1945, I inserted a letter in the *Church Times* as follows:

> Sir,
>
> I am very anxious to trace a clerical ghost story which is not in Lord Halifax's two collections. As long as it was attributed to the late Mgr. Benson, it could be discounted, as he professed to make up his ghost stories; but I cannot find it in his works. I can only trace it second-hand to a deceased Anglican priest, whose name I cannot get.
>
> It is the story of children (with mediumistic gifts) hiding under an ancient table and hearing the words of the Latin Mass, which they repeated. The table was then found to have been an emergency altar used in penal times.
>
> Is there any record or parallel of this story, which seems new in the ghost lore of the Church?

To this I received a number of answers:

Miss M. N. Kennedy of Northiam sent me a version in the script of her friend Miss Edith Pippet as follows:

About 24 years ago an Anglican priest—long since dead—a friend for whose veracity I can vouch—told me the following experience. He was taking duty for the summer at an Episcopal Church in Scotland and was staying in the Presbytery with his family. It was their custom to have tea in the study and after tea the children spent till bedtime with them there. Soon he noticed that the children made for the largish refectory-looking table which stood in the centre of the room and which the Rector used as his desk. They remained apparently absorbed in some interest of their own *under* the table and completely quiet.

One evening my friend was reading when suddenly his attention was arrested by the sound of the children repeating in rhythmical sonorous Latin the Canon of the Mass.

"What are you saying?" he asked in amazement.

"We are saying what the table teaches us," was the reply. Then they told him how the first night they had gone under the table to hide and had heard the table talking, and how after that they had gone each time to listen and had at last learnt what it said. The children knew no Latin at all and had never even heard a Latin Mass, so it was obvious that the table had taught them what they were saying.

My friend, with the approval of the Rector, got in touch with experts who came and examined the table. They found a false top had been superimposed. Below was the wooden frame with the stone *mensa* inset—the five crosses intact. The belief was that it had been needed for secret Roman Masses long after the Reformation. How it came to the Presbytery could not be traced.

The story of echoes descending through material media from the days of persecution occurs in Roger Pater's *Mystic Voices* (Burns and Oates, 1923). A story called "The Persecution Chalice" covers this type of mystical experience which is also told of several tables and old hiding places: the return of sounds recognizable as of a priest saying Mass. It is impossible to disintegrate the core of authentic occurrence from the legend which has gathered round it.

Anything which has played a part in events that saturated, as it were, with the emotions involved. So much so, that it can influence people of exceptional sympathetic powers and enable them to perceive the original events, more or less perfectly, as if they were re-enacted before them.

Mr. J. W. Sowan wrote:

An Anglican clergyman, many years ago, told me an anecdote which is a slight variant of the one related by you under the above heading in the *Church Times* of the 9th. This good priest is no longer living.

A priest (whether Roman or Anglican I do not know and it does not matter) was visiting friends who lived in a country house which had either been a monastery liquidated by the unspeakable Bluff King Hal, or was built on the site of one such.

During the evening, the children of the house asked their mother if they might go upstairs and "listen to the singing."

"What is that?" enquired the priest. "Oh," replied the mother, "they say they can hear singing up in their nursery, but of course it is all nonsense."

"I am not so sure about that," replied the priest. "May I go up too?"

"Of course, but nobody else has ever heard it." He went up and on enquiry elicited from the children that it was "funny music and they could not understand the words." He asked them, when it commenced, to try and sing to him what they could hear, and they did so.

On returning to the mother he said, "What your children can hear, but I could not, is the monks who lived here five hundred years ago or so, singing their Evening Office. It is in Latin and to the ancient plainsong."

Can wood or parchment convey echoes from the past? The great Catholic Liturgist Edmund Bishop once wrote to Dean Armitage Robinson:

I say don't laugh: because being Devonshire born and what is more deeply felt, I have a sense of superstitious realism as to ghosts ... and that spirit touches spirit still though centuries divide us. ... Do please, before you send me to the Limbo of Fanciful Nonsensicality read *In Memoriam* XCV ... you see I feel, that is to say in the days when actually handled (and conversed with) certain MSS that, scrutinizing them, one came into contact with the living writer or originator of them!

A curious experience with a parallel auditory hallucination occurs in *Farming Adventure*, by Wentworth Day, in connection with the ruined Priory of the Canons of the Holy Sepulchre at Thetford in Norfolk:

> It was in this old house, sitting one bright May morning at 11 o'clock, that my host and hostess, Dr. and Mrs. Jameson heard, in 1937, the sweet singing of ghostly monks. It was so clear on the air that they thought at first that the wireless was turned on. But there was no wireless. And for half an hour the monks of 700 years ago sang sweetly. Then came slow reading by a man's voice. Silence, and then the ringing regular footsteps of a man walking on a paved floor: There are green grasses, fig trees lucent against roofless walls. ...
>
> That is a strange story but no stranger than was told me a week earlier by Robert Fuller, of Spinney Abbey in Cambridgeshire. He, his two sons, and a maidservant, at breakfast on Low Sunday morning after Easter seven years ago, under a blue sky, heard suddenly the sweet unearthly singing of monks in Latin. They, too, at first thought it was the wireless. But there is no wireless. "It was high up in the air, ten or fifteen feet above the ground, the sweetest singing I have ever heard," said Mr. Fuller. "I know no Latin, but I do know English and this was not English. It was over there," and he waved his hand.
>
> "And what was once over there?" I said. "That's where the old chapel once stood. We've traced out the walls and the foundations."

XV: THE PRIEST WHO HAD A LOOK AT HIS SUCCESSOR

A VERY interesting case occurred some forty years ago in the diocese of Southwark. It was told to me by Canon Cooksey very simply and seems to need no further verification.

On December 3, 1908, I was living with Dr. Amigo (Bishop of Southwark) in St George's Road. On the previous evening we dined together and after dinner he went to his room and I to mine on the third floor. On my way to say Mass the following morning I passed an elderly man at the foot of the stairs leading from my floor. He was unknown to me but wearing a cassock and cotta. He had grey hair and a long upper lip. He stood with his hands joined and his head on one side looking in an inquiring way at me. I took him for some priest who had arrived overnight and was looking for the Bishop's Chapel in which to say Mass. I would have spoken to him but he vanished completely. There was no finding him but I remembered his features. I went upstairs twice and descended in the same way to satisfy myself it was not some trick of the light shining from the street. But I saw no more of the figure I felt was of a living man.

At breakfast I asked the Bishop if there was a visiting priest but no. At luncheon the Bishop told me that a telegram had arrived to say the Parish Priest of Bromley, Father Ford, had died at six-thirty that morning. It was the hour I had risen to say Mass. I did not know Father Ford by sight and it meant nothing to me till six weeks later when I was appointed by the Bishop to succeed him at Bromley. Soon after, I entered a parishioner's house, where there was hanging the photograph of an elderly priest. Without the least doubt, it was the man I had met on the stairs on December 3rd. When I asked who it was I was told: "Don't you know that was dear Father Ford!"

Canon Cooksey confirmed this experience to me (10th May 1947). The story had already appeared without names in *Apparitions and Haunted Houses* by Sir Ernest Bennett with a foreword by the Dean of St Paul's, where the details are more numerous, with this comment by the Canon (as well as a second experience):

> There are one or two points to be noticed. (1) The apparition was straight in front of me. (2) The subject of the apparition was entirely unknown to me. (3) At the relevant date there was no thought of my being appointed to a parish. (4) Although the only light was through the windows from the street lamps, I saw every detail of this apparition quite clearly. (5) At this time I was in my 38th year and had not had any previous occult experience.

Canon Cooksey's second experience was this:

> Early in the year 1909 I visited a house in the Bromley Common district (Kent) as an ordinary parochial visit. I had not been to the house before and the inhabitants were not known to me. It was a small house in a row of houses in a lesser residential district. The wife of the tenant opened the door and, as I spoke to her on entering, I saw behind her an elderly woman with grey hair who wore a cap and was a typical woman of the class of the inhabitants. I was shown into the parlour by my hostess—who excused herself for a few minutes as she said she was doing some cooking for her husband's meal when he returned from the city about 5:20. She then said:
>
> "You know he goes up to town by a very early train and generally gets back between five and six. It's terribly lonely for me now all day by myself. Up till three weeks ago I had an old lady living with me and she was company—but she died three

weeks ago. Since my husband went out this morning I have not spoken to a living soul till you called."

XVI: THE PENITENT SUICIDE

I AM indebted to Father Coghlin, O.S.B., of St. Gregory's Priory, Cheltenham, for an interesting story which he heard first-hand from Father Flint, of the Northampton Diocese:

Father Flint was sent as a curate to High Wycombe to form a mission. It was necessary for him to live in a labourer's cottage. One day a hunting man, dressed in pink, walked in, as the Hunt had killed in the neighbourhood. He said he had ridden over the county border from Oxfordshire, as he lived in an old house his father had bought. Realizing that Father Flint was a Catholic priest he invited him to come and stay with him and say Mass, whenever he had a few days off, for the house he inhabited had belonged to an old Catholic family.

In time he found the opportunity of taking such a holiday, and was given an attic in which to sleep. At the foot of the bed was a rocking chair. He found he was sleeping with difficulty, owing to the great oppression which he felt. He was woken by the rocking of the chair, but found it had been moved to the front of the fire. He rose and replaced it, but was woken up again, and once again he saw it rocking in front of the fire. This happened several times before he finally procured sleep.

In the morning his host told him the history of the house. It had been occupied by the last of a long Catholic line, who had gambled away house and fortune and, after losing the last *coup*, had ridden back to shoot himself at home. While he was dying, his faithful old servant pulled him on to a chair in front of the fire and then tried to fetch a priest. This proved impossible in those days, and the old servant could only say the prayers for the dying. He died very penitently in the chair before any priest could be found.

"And I wish I knew which was the room!" said Father Flint's host. "Oh, I think I can tell you that," replied Father Flint.

114

Incidentally, Father Coghlin had a curious experience himself while staying at Castle Acton, near Penzance, with the late Catholic Ranee of Sarawak. At four in the morning he was awakened by an electric bell which twice rang violently outside his room. When he told his story in the morning he was told: "Old Mrs. Unwin's nurse-slept there and a bell was placed there for night calls in case Mrs. Unwin was taken ill. But after she died, it was moved."

Perhaps Mrs. Unwin rang for what might well be her need in the next world.

XVII: A SPIRIT ATTENDS MIDNIGHT MASS

S IR ERNEST BENNETT in his *Apparitions and Haunted Houses* gave a case of distinctly Catholic interest:

> For the following case I am indebted to Dr. Eustace of Crossbush, Arundel, Chairman of the Arundel Bench of Magistrates (March 4th, 1934).
>
> For some months, my wife's health had caused anxiety and in December 1932, a serious operation had become imperative. It was performed on December 21st, in a Hove nursing home. As an operation, it was a brilliant success, but three days later, sign of heart failure developed. At 11:50 p.m. on December 24th, she became unconscious and at 3:15 a.m. on Christmas morning, she died. In accordance with her previously expressed wish, I alone was with her. I brought her body home—to the home she loved. Then on the evening of the 25th to St Philip's Church, Arundel, where it lay until after the Requiem Mass on the 28th, when I buried her in the grave she herself had chosen beside that of our son.
>
> For some six weeks after her death I remained quite certain that her spirit still lived and that we should meet again. These doubts concerning survival after death began to assert themselves, as had often been the case with me in the past years. Gradually I reached a state of disquieting uncertainty, when I could only trust the larger hope and finally I lost even that slender stay. I strove to recapture my former certitude but failing to do so I resigned myself to the loss of that on which I had leaned so heavily and faced the duties of the day as best I could, realizing that on a lee shore life had dragged its anchor. A week or two later the event which I now relate, took place. The impression left by it is still so vivid that I have not the slightest difficulty in recalling the details.

Shortly before sundown, I was walking in the wood at the rear of this house with my wife's sister, who has lived with us for many years. We had been looking at the seedling trees which my wife had planted before she was taken ill. I remarked on how gratified she would have been to see how well they were doing. Her sister replied: "I'm quite sure that she does know, and that she often comes to see them." I said nothing, for I did not wish to shake a faith which I had ceased to share. We returned to the garden which lies in front of the house, my sister-in-law turning east to shut up the chickens, and I to the west, for the purpose of closing the shutters over the French windows of the drawing-room. As I made my way along the path in front of the house, I was not thinking of my wife but of a neighbour to whom I had sent some valuable books, and as I walked, I was picturing his pleasure on opening the parcel. As I reached the rose garden, on which the drawing-room windows open, I came instinctively to an immediate halt, for standing on the lawn beyond the rose garden, and less than thirty yards from me, was my wife. She stood looking straight at me as though she had been expecting me. Her face and figure were as distinct and clear-cut as in life. She wore no hat and the slight evening breeze did not ruffle her hair or disturb the folds of her dress. She was clad in a perfectly fitting soft grey gown, which reflected the shadows thrown on it by the pergola behind her, but I noticed that her dress did not conform to the prevailing fashion in that it reached almost to her feet and that, although covering her neck and shoulders, it had no collar or definite upper line of demarcation. Her arms hung naturally on either side but were not in contact with her hips and she wore no gloves. She looked in perfect health, but what struck me most was the expression with which she regarded me. Steadily, without change of aspect, she gazed intently at me without suggestion of either joy or sorrow, but with a puzzled look of remonstrance as though she were surprised and disappointed with me over something which I was doing and from which she wished me to desist. Translated into words her expression would well have been rendered by: "How stupid of you! Why so foolish?" The vision lasted a full minute at least. I was fully aware throughout that it was a vision, for, although I believe that I smiled and that my face reflected my joy at seeing her, I made no attempt to speak or to approach her. With her eyes still meeting mine, she faded from my sight—not suddenly, but quite gradually.

The immediate conclusion I drew was that I had been the victim of an hallucination, that presently I should begin to hear voices and would finally succumb to an attack of delusional insanity. Although I felt quite normal, this thought perturbed me and so that evening, after supper, I confided to my sister-in-law what had happened. To this she at once replied:

"I quite forgot to tell you that yesterday, as I came from church [she belongs to the Church of England and attends St Nicolas Parish Church, Arundel] Mrs. Welch, coming from Mass at St Philip's, stopped me and said she wanted to say something to me." [Mrs. Welch is an elderly lady and much crippled, but a very well-read and matter-of-fact person. My wife had made her acquaintance through attending St. Philip's and had often assisted Mrs. Welch to her pew. My sister-in-law, however, knew her only very slightly.]

Mrs. Welch's narrative, as told to Miss Orme:

I went to the midnight service at the Convent of Poor Clares, Crossbush, on Christmas Eve. I got to the church at five minutes to twelve. On entering it, I saw that the seat I usually occupy, as it is easy of access, was already taken. I turned to find another as near at hand as possible. As I did so, your sister (Mrs. Eustace) came to me, took my arm as she had often done, and helped me to a vacant seat. When I went up to the chancel steps, she came with me and helped me down and up from my knees, and then assisted me back to my seat. I do not remember her leaving me, but when I got up to go, she had already gone. I had not seen her for six months, but I had heard that she had not been well enough to attend St. Philip's. I had heard nothing of her being seriously ill, or of her having gone to Brighton for any operation. I returned home after the service quite convinced that I had seen her in church and that she had helped me as she had often done, but I was surprised at not seeing her at the end of the service, for I wanted to thank her. I attended Mass at St. Philip's on Christmas morning. It was a great shock to me when the priest announced her death. Thus I knew that it was her spirit which was in the church at the service on Christmas Eve and that it had come to help me.

Please note that it was at 11:55 on Christmas Eve, 1932, that my wife was seen by Mrs. Welch at Crossbush. At that moment I was standing by her bedside in the nursing home at Hove. It was then that she became unconscious and I noted the time by the clock which was on a small table nearby.

My wife has not appeared to me again. I do not anticipate that she will do so. I am more than satisfied. I am well content to leave that interpretation to others, for I know now that I know.

Mrs. Welch's narrative, as told to Mr. Eustace:

It was as I approached the step leading to the compartment where the priest was waiting to hear individual confessions that I first saw Mrs. Eustace. She was standing by the step waiting her turn to go in. She bowed to me and smiled as was her wont and she gave that slight movement sideways of her shoulders which was peculiar to her. I had not the slightest doubt of her identity. She put her hand under mine and helped me up the step as she had often done in the past. I had not seen her since the previous January. I was glad to see her there at that hour, for I knew that it meant that she must be feeling strong and well. She again came to me, again took my arm and assisted me over the floor, which is very slippery. I believe that I managed with her assistance to kneel at the rails. She was holding my hand and helping me, but whether or not I did actually get down on my knees I cannot now be positive. I had heard nothing of her for many months. I did not know that she had been taken ill and had gone to Brighton. When my maid told me on Christmas morning that Mrs. Eustace was dead, I replied: "That cannot be true. There must be some mistake. She was at the Midnight Mass and helped me along both to the confessional and again to the chancel rails." I have since tried to persuade myself that the whole thing was some trick of my imagination, but I have not been able to do so. I was not thinking of her when I went to the Chapel. No thought of her came to me until I saw her standing by the step leading to the confessional and I remain convinced that it was she and no one else who was there, who bowed and smiled as we met and who took my hand and assisted me both then and later along the floor and at the rails. I am quite clear about the whole matter.

It is interesting to note that in this account the first apparition occurred at or near the moment of death, the second some weeks afterwards. Mrs. Welch is a careful witness and is absolutely convinced that her experience was not a case of mistaken identity.

All the same it is not clear whether Mrs. Welch heard of her friend's death from her maid or from the priest on

Christmas morning—possibly from both. She mentions different periods of time as elapsing since she saw her friend in the flesh, though this would not discredit her main story. Father Basil Curwen wrote to me (1st October 1945):

> I knew Dr. Eustace rather well. He died a few weeks ago. He never told me your story. He was a Protestant and I should have thought with little or no faith, though a charming man; chairman of the local Bench and a good one. He procured Mass for his wife from time to time and always attended the service. His property lies alongside the Poor Clares' ground at Cross Bush, a hamlet just over a mile east of Arundel. Eustace's wife and son (also dead) became Catholics.

XVIII: THE SHREWSBURY DEATH WARNING

UNTIL 1856 the Premier Earldom of England was Catholic. With the death of Bertram, the 17th Earl of Shrewsbury, the title passed to distant Protestant cousins. John, the 16th Earl, the great church-builder and patron of Pugin, died in 1852. His issue was confined to daughters, who became princesses in Rome. His heir was his nephew Bertram in whom he hoped to renew the Catholic descent, but this was not to be: and the story relates to the warning offered from the other side.

Dr. F. A. Paley was a son of Archdeacon Paley of the *Christian Evidences*, an eminent classical Editor and a Catholic convert. He had been engaged as tutor to the heir when he saw the ghost in the late Forties. Many years later he passed the story to the historian Sir Charles Oman, who was interested together with an Oxford group in such supernatural happenings. Sir Charles furnished me with a copy of Dr. Paley's communication, writing from Frewin Hall, Oxford (15th May 1946):

> Enclosed please find Dr. Paley's declaration. It seems to me that the weak point is that Bertram Talbot died much later than a year after 1848. The apparition was far too long before the disaster. Dr. Paley was intensely interested in all things occult and a very old man when he sent me the story.

> [In our opinion the apparition was sufficiently warranted as a warning of the early death hovering over the heir. There was still

a chance of protecting his health, but though he succeeded to the title he proved to be the last of his line.]

Apthorp Boscombe
Bournemouth (July 17th 1883)

In the year 1847-8 I was residing at Alton Towers in the family of the late John, 16th Earl of Shrewsbury. I was then tutor to his nephew and heir Bertram Talbot, then aged 17-18.

One evening my pupil and I were riding home somewhat late, the dusk having just set in. We were on a road about a mile from the Towers, on the left hand bounded by a canal (if I rightly remember) and on the right by a rather steep bank, thickly set with oak-trees of considerable size and age.

My attention was drawn to a figure of a woman (as I thought) and somewhat like a gypsy, looking at us with her head bent forward; her body being concealed by an oak tree. I called my pupil's attention to her, and he distinctly saw her. Knowing that the place was solitary and the value of the life in my charge, I decided to go up to the spot and question this strange intruder.

I dismounted, and while my pupil held my horse, climbed up the bank to the tree, perhaps 20 yards off. To my very great surprise no one was to be seen, I returned and asked my pupil if he felt quite sure that he had seen the figure. "Quite certain," he said and he thought that she had something like a handkerchief over her head.

On returning I related to Lady Shrewsbury the particulars. I at once saw that I had disturbed her very much, and though there was company in the house, she declined to appear at dinner. In the evening, the Chaplain came to me and reproached me for having— innocently of course—caused alarm in the family.

It seems that there was a family tradition that had been carefully concealed from the young Bertram, that the apparition of a woman always preceded the death of an heir.

Well, the fine young lad, on whose life an ancient title and large estate depended, did die a year (or it may be more) after we had seen that strange appearance.

Of course, it may have been an optical delusion of some kind, but the family tradition, verified in this case by the countess, is certainly curious. Bertram had succeeded to the Earldom by the death of his uncle before he himself was carried off by consumption.

XIX: THE GHOSTS OF BESFORD COURT

THE following was communicated by Monsignor Thomas Newsome.

The only ghost I have ever seen at Besford or indeed in my whole life, although I have had experiences in another haunted house, was an "elemental." These are described profusely in psychic literature. An elemental is first cousin to a poltergeist, which is a thing like a mischievous schoolboy gone mad and which hurls objects about and sometimes injures human beings.

Our elemental is round about the Dower House and only at very rare intervals makes its presence seen. Many years ago my step-sister, Mrs. Brown, was gravely injured in a motor accident and her mother came to look after her. Both slept in the room in the Dower House in the southeast corner. Mr. Webb happened to be staying the night and we both went to bed early. This is the story I heard next morning. My step-mother knocked at my door, but knocked so gently that she failed to rouse me. Consequently, she went to Mr. Webbs' room and knocked on his door and he awoke immediately. She explained to him there was a big light in the study, that it was streaming across the lawn and lighting up the trunk and lower branches of the beech tree on the edge of the further lawn.

At that time our principal sources of illumination were two candelabra, each carrying three candles. We took them in to our evening meal and we brought them back into the study. That night as usual we had blown them out and taken our bedroom candles to light us to bed. Where was the light coming from? Mr. Webb said he would get up and look but as there was no sound of his coming down from his room during the next ten minutes, my step-mother went back and asked the reason, thinking he had fallen asleep again. Mr. Webb said he was just getting his clothes on. Later, he emerged properly clad, and asking my step-mother to stand at the top of the stairs in case anyone tried to get upstairs, he went down very circumspectly to the study door. He soon returned saying there was no light in the study and that he had looked through the keyhole. My stepmother went back to her bedroom and she and Brown saw that the light was still streaming out from the windows. After about five minutes it suddenly vanished. Next day on hearing the story I invited them all to examine the door of the study. There was no keyhole.

About a year later two visitors were sitting in front of the fire, the six candles being alight in the centre of the table. They both saw a dense black shadow, with the outline of a woman with a headgear something like that of a nun, pass slowly across the whitewashed wall above the fireplace. This shadow could not have come from the candles which were stationary or from the fire which is immediately under the shadow, neither could it have been cast by either of the two sitting figures or from anything else in the room. They were not merely impressed, they were actually startled.

About three years later it was reported to me that a queer unearthly face had been seen pressed against a window in the kitchen and that on noticing that it was observed it had withdrawn and disappeared. I attached no importance to this but about four years later I myself went into the lowest lavatory and saw at a distance of about two feet a hypoplastic face looking at me—the eyes were round and opened wide, the nose was a lump, and the mouth a line, the face itself was round. We looked at one another for about twenty seconds and the face then slowly receded. It corresponds with the face of what is known as an elemental.

It must be remembered that the site of Besford Court and its immediate environment has on account of its natural advantages been the centre of human life for many thousands of years. There was a great house there at the time of the Norman Conquest. In Saxon times, Beoff, who built a bigger house than previously existed, gave his name to the ford across Bow Brook and to the district adjoining that ford. The early Anglo-Saxons were here, as we know from the graveyard in which their skeletons were found. The Romans had a station here and the ramparts of their stockaded camp still exist in the Roman Field. A site that appealed to them would appeal to earlier settlers and the fertile vale of Evesham must have made a good place of settlement to the Paleolithic men.

Things and influences linger on in spite of Christianity in these ancient abodes of the human race. Concentrations of humanity together acting as spiritual forces tend either to wipe them out or else to irritate them into making final efforts. We are immersed in a world of unseen realities. To me, it is marvellous how seldom the barriers of the two worlds are broken down or how rarely we in this world of solid homely things are forced to admit the existence of a preternatural world that for the most part is hindered from making its existence and proximity. Mr. Charles Burke has been a member of our staff of masters for a number of years. His evidence is as follows:

"On an evening in October in the year 1928 I was sitting in the masters' common room with Mr. McAllister. We were both facing the fire but my chair was further back than his. There was a lull in the conversation. I happened to glance round toward the door of the billiard room. Against the right jamb of the door, a figure of a woman—a , white misty sort of figure but very clearly outlined—she appeared to be dressed in what I would term eighteenth-century costume, with a bustle and a sunbonnet, a bodice with buttons down the front. She wore her hair in ringlets clustered on each side of the bonnet and underneath. The features were indistinguishable but the whole thing gave me the impression of a gentlewoman about 30. As I stared, with open mouth, at the apparition, she turned half right and went through the door, which was closed, sideways. At this moment Mr. McAllister turned round and saw my open mouth. We then took the time, it was two minutes past twelve. We searched the common room and rooms round about and found or saw nothing more.

(Signed) C. BURKE."

When Father Stanbridge was at Besford his bedsitting-room was on the ground floor. His room is now used as the Court Office. He told me that at least on one occasion he turned out all the lights but that during the night the lights were turned on, and several things happened which caused him to wonder whether or not members of the staff or boys were playing tricks. I do not remember that this suspicion was ever confirmed.

When Mr. and Mrs. McAllister's baby was baptized, Miss Carnegie gave us all a cup of tea in her sitting-room which was the queer corner room upstairs in the old part. A master, by the way, had this as his room for some time and although he said nothing we wondered after he had left at finding two long cudgels at the head of his bed, ready to hand as though he expected something to attack him. After tea, most of us went over to the Dower House, and as a new-born baby is sometimes an interruption to conversation, Mrs. McAllister remained behind with the baby in the room. Here, in her own words, is what happened:

"After being in the room alone with my baby for about five minutes the light went out and I got up to turn it on. I found some difficulty in getting at the switch as though something was pushing against my hand. The door in the meantime had opened. I then succeeded in getting the light on and closed the door. I sat down again by the fire. Almost immediately the same thing happened again: the door unlatched itself, which could not happen without pressure on the latch, and the light went out. I put the light on this time without experiencing any difficulty and then shut the door. I felt there was somebody near me but I could see nothing. When Miss Dinley came in a little later I asked her whether she had been playing any tricks. This she denied, and indeed such tricks would be quite out of place, and also under the circumstances idiotic. Moreover, had she been dodging about on the creaky boards outside the door, I certainly should have heard her. She is not a person who one would ever suspect of such peculiar pranks.
(Signed) EILEEN McALLISTER."

Mrs. McAllister signed her statement, but as she had thought things over and spoken with Miss Kate Dinley, added the following letter.

"Greenways"
29.1.34

"MONSIGNOR,
"Regarding the enclosed, Kate reminded me that she was actually in the room with me when the incidents occurred, and I questioned her about turning the lights off, etc., and everything happened as stated.
"I believe now that I had mixed this incident up with a similar occurrence. Some months later, I was in the same room alone with baby, waiting for Miss Carnegie to return from her office which is downstairs; and the lights suddenly went out, and the door unlatched, and I had the same idea that someone was there but saw nothing and heard nothing, and I had difficulty in switching on the light again.
"This incident happened on the night of a Boxing Tournament, and I believe that Miss Carnegie and myself were

about the only two people in the Court who were not present so I know that it was nobody playing any tricks on me.

EILEEN McALLISTER."

From the various stories I have heard I conclude that children have a fascination for the Grey Lady and there is an odd story current, the origin of which appears to be unknown, that the Grey Lady's own baby died under distressing circumstances in the corner room. The story of the district is that in the annex of this corner room a particular spot indicated by tradition, the child was murdered.

XX: THE ORATORY GHOST-STORY

VERSIONS of this famous story have appeared in Lord Halifax's *Ghost Book* and in the *Westminster Cathedral Chronicle*.

The London Oratorians vouch for the story as may appear by some correspondence. The late Father Vincent Baker (R.I.P.), who had been at a Private School called Ludgrove with me, wrote (25th January 1944):

> I can tell you about the apparition here, as Father Edward Crewse told it me himself—not what I should call a ghost—presumably, the lady's guardian angel. I have recently read *The most haunted house in England*, I can't quite see why they didn't do what they were asked to—have Masses said. According to the stories one hears, ghosts usually want something done—body buried in consecrated ground, slanderous letters destroyed. Father John Talbot had hectic stories about Hever Castle (or the Down House) and what happened to him himself and even more to Father Martindale. I wonder if Father Thurston had any things on *Poltergeists*. I find it very difficult (impossible) to deny their existence. If they appear for some purpose (as above) it is understandable. The murderous or destructive ones are more difficult to explain.

And in another letter:

> The Oratory ghost wasn't a ghost, if by that one means the apparition of a dead person. It was the apparition of a living person viz. Father Basevi. Whenever I write to you, I think of singing *Lead, Kindly Light* at Ludgrove— "whom I have known long since and lost awhile."

Father Vincent's references to Borley Rectory will appeal to Catholics. The traditions there were distinctly of the old Faith. The Waldegraves were patrons of Borley Rectory and Manor. Sir Edward Waldegrave was sent to the Tower for allowing Mass at Borley. Dom Richard Whitehouse, a Benedictine, was present when a message appeared on the wall to "get Light, Mass and Prayers."

One quotation from the official account of the hauntings may be made: "The repeated appeals for Requiem Mass, prayers, etc., all suggest a young Catholic girl in distress. There was absolute quiet during Holy Week and usually on Sundays."

Now for the Oratory story.

Father William Munster, the Superior, wrote to me from the Oratory:

> Yes, by all means use the "Oratory Telephone" Story for your new book if you think it of sufficient interest. Father Edward Crewse, now dead, was the priest who was summoned and who gave the lady the last sacraments. The priest who he imagined woke him up to tell him there was a call, was Father Lionel Basevi [who has since died a holy death]. He wrote an account of the incident for the Psychical Society. Perhaps you have come across it. As far as I remember the account in Lord Halifax's book is substantially correct.
>
> I remember the occurrence very well as I was here at the time. I think it happened in the late autumn of 1918 and just before Father Vincent joined us. What is perhaps worth recording is that Father Crewse was an extremely matter-of-fact man, the very last person to imagine things. And I remember so well his saying that it was not until he was kept waiting a long time on the steps of the house in Ennismore Gardens that he thought anything odd had occurred. But he was so firmly convinced Father Basevi had awakened him that he apologized to him for his brusqueness the next morning. The nurse, who opened the door to him, looked very surprised but in answer to his question replied that she supposed the night nurse had telephoned for him.

As the story had some publicity Mgr. Coote went to the

Oratory to enquire:

I went to the Oratory to enquire, with a view to publishing an account of it in the *Westminster Cathedral Chronicle*. I was fortunate enough to have the full details related to me by the priest concerned in the story, in the very bed-sitting-room in which the incident occurred. Readers may therefore be assured that the following account is true in every detail as described to me by the Oratorian Father in question.

One afternoon a short time ago Fr. Crewse was requested to visit a lady who was ill. When he arrived at her house he met the doctor, who very urgently requested him not to administer the last rites at that particular moment, but to be satisfied with giving the patient a few cheering words. He very reluctantly consented but, when he had seen the lady, greatly regretted his promise and the fact that the doctor should have made such a request, as he feared that the patient was very much worse than the doctor had led him to understand. However, his promise had been given; so he arranged that he would come again in the morning and administer the Last Sacraments. But before he left the house he gave the nurse his telephone number and asked her to telephone should the patient become suddenly worse before the morning. She promised to do so.

As usual, that night the telephone was switched on to one of the Father's rooms, as is the custom at the Oratory, with a view to any possible sick-calls. Fr. Crewse retired to bed at his usual hour after reciting his rosary, in which he did not forget to include his patient of the afternoon.

In the early hours of the morning he was startled out of a deep sleep by his bedroom door opening, and he clearly saw, by the light of the moon through his open, uncovered window, a medium-sized, dark-robed figure standing by it. He understood the person to be saying something about a sick-call.

"For heaven's sake, man," he hastily answered, sitting up in bed and rubbing his eyes, not quite sure if it was the Father on duty or the lodge-porter, "do speak clearly."

"Be quick!" came the reply in clearer tones. "There is no time to lose. There is a telephone message."

"Right—right you are!" at once answered Fr. Crewse, as he threw back the bed-clothes. The word "telephone" brought back in an instant to his mind the sick-call of the previous afternoon, and it did not therefore occur to him to ask for the address. He sprang out of bed—the door closing as he did so—and turned on the light, observing at the same time that it was just on the quarter to four o'clock. He quickly dressed, and went to the chapel for the Holy Oils and the Blessed Sacrament, remarking, on the way, at the forgetfulness of his caller to turn on the light for him.

Making his way swiftly across the space between the house and the gates that shut it off from the main road, he found them locked, as they should be, and had to knock up the lodge-porter to let him out. Within a minute or two he was well on his way to the house he had visited the previous afternoon, and as he waited after his first ring at the bell and congratulated himself on his smart arrival, he looked at his watch and saw that it still wanted five minutes to four. He rang again—and again. A clock in the vicinity chimed the hour. He rang and knocked.

"Strange that there is no one ready to answer the door after telephoning," he thought. In the stillness of the moonlight night it seemed to him that he was making noise enough to wake the dead. The dead! Could the worst have happened? His regret of yesterday came upon him with sudden force, so that he became alarmed. He banged at the door. The electric light was on in the hall and up the stairs, as he could see. He knew that there were only six people in the house—the sick lady in one room, her husband, given up as hopeless, in another, two day nurses (now evidently in a sound sleep), and the two night nurses in attendance on the patients. The children had all safely recovered from influenza and had been taken elsewhere.

A cat on the other side of the road gave forth at frequent intervals a doleful howl in the still, cold night. ... He waited impatiently. It was impossible to go back after that telephone call, but it was strange that he should be kept waiting like this.

He rang once again furiously. The peal seemed to reverberate through the whole house. He looked at his watch—it was twelve minutes past four! What if that soul should miss the last rites of the Church! Would he not be at fault? It was a heavy anxiety.

He thought he would get a stone and throw it at one of the lighted windows above. Again, the cat desecrated the still night with its unnerving moan. The priest could bear it no longer. As though driving off some evil, hovering spirit, he threw the stone with all his force in the direction of the cat. Its uncanny cry stopped abruptly. A clock chimed the quarter past. At last to the priest's great relief, the door opened.

"Come in, doctor," said a nurse; "I fear you have been kept waiting."

"I am not the doctor; I'm a priest."

"Oh, I suppose they telephoned for you? That's bad news. Will you go up?"

Fr. Crewse made his way up to the sick room, and as he quietly entered he saw the nurse kneeling by the bedside and noticed that she was very startled at seeing him. He also heard the sick person saying:

"I do wish Father Crewse would come."

As he learnt afterwards, for about half an hour before his arrival the lady had been expressing an earnest desire to see him. The nurse, however, not being a Catholic, and not realizing that a priest would come outside the ordinary hours, suggested that she should recite some prayers with her patient from a Catholic prayerbook. Fr. Crewse arrived while the nurse was doing this. He at once gave the lady the Last Sacraments, much to her relief and peace of mind. Within an hour or two she became unconscious. After reciting the prayers for the dying, the priest prepared to leave the house.

"Thank you so much for coming so opportunely," said the nurse, "but you quite startled me." "On the contrary, thanks are due to you for telephoning."

"Oh, but I didn't."

"Well, someone did. I expect it was Mrs. P.'s sister."

As the nurses were not Catholics, the priest took it that one of the lady's relations had telephoned in their anxiety about her condition. Fr. Crewse heard that she died a few hours later. She became a Catholic at the age of eighteen, and been an exemplary one up to her edifying death at the age of thirty-two.

In the evening of the same day, Fr. Crewse had occasion to speak to the Father whose duty it had been to answer the telephone, and in the course of conversation said:

"By the way, I'm sorry I spoke to you so sharply last night."

"Why, when do you mean?"

"When you came to call me."

"But I *never called you last night*!"

"My dear Father, you came to my room at a quarter to four this morning and told me there was a telephone sick-call."

"I never left my room last night. I had a sleepless night and was awake at that time: I happened to notice the time because I had my light on. And what is more, *there was no telephone call last night*!"

In the foregoing story, it should be borne in mind that Fr. Crewse had no reason, up to the moment he spoke to the Father responsible for the night telephone, to suppose that anything unusual had happened. He had a sick-call in the afternoon and intended to return to see the patient the following morning in the ordinary way. He mentioned the sick person in his prayers as was his wont in such cases. He made no special preparation before going to bed. He was awakened by his door being suddenly opened. He took the caller to be the Father on duty, and were it not that he knew it could not have been the lodge porter, because he had had to arouse him from sleep, he would not have spoken to the Father at all. It was only because he presumed the Father had called him, that he referred to the sick-call at all when speaking to him on other business. On enquiry at the Telephone Exchange it was stated that there was no record of any call for the Oratory on the night in question.

"I suppose that is what one would call a case of telepathy," remarked the nurse afterwards.

"I don't know," answered the priest, "but I do know that I saw you on your knees praying when I entered the room and heard Mrs. P. asking for me, that somehow I was called by someone, and that Mrs. P. had the happiness of receiving the Last Sacraments just in time."

(The foregoing is reprinted from the *Westminster Cathedral Chronicle*.)

As Father Crewse's name has been given it is possible to give that of his penitent—a Mrs. Ponsonby. The account he gave to Lord Halifax is identical, except that he thought he saw the white collar of an Oratorian in the moonlight round the neck of his visitor. However, the question remains, as Mgr. Coote wrote—

"Who called the Priest?"

A parallel case was given by the late Canon Vere of St. Patrick's, Soho Square, who was summoned to attend a young man, in a lodging house. It appeared that he had not sent for the priest, but confessing he was a Catholic promised to come to Communion in the morning. He died during the night. Canon Vere believed he had been summoned by the ghost of his mother.

XXI: AN ABBOT'S GHOST STORIES

1. The Spectral Face at Liberton

ABBOT Sir David Hunter-Blair, O.S.B., was very critical of Lord Halifax's *Ghost Book* and especially of the account given by Mrs. MacLagan, wife of the Archbishop of York, which he considered "both inadequate and unsatisfactory and she does not even make the remotest allusion to the real secret of Glamis or to the two traditions as to what that secret really is." However, Sir David published in the *Universe* a first-hand account of another Scottish Ghost—"The Spectral Face of Liberton," which he had investigated with the Marquess of Bute, who had an occult feeling as strong as his Catholic belief. Many years ago, the late Marquess of Bute, who was deeply interested in things psychic and one of the founders of the Psychical Society, gave me a very remarkable photograph, which had impressed him greatly, as it did me also.

It represents a hall, or chamber, of the ancient house of Liberton, in the Midlothian parish of the same name.

Liberton House, not being occupied by the owner, has been frequently let; and it was a tenant of the place who got a professional photographer (this is an important point) to take the photograph. It has several interesting features: the ancient nail-studded door framed in stone; a similarly-framed recess above; a William-and-Mary chair against the wall, and a long two-handled sword leaning in the corner.

But when the photograph had been duly developed, there appeared on the top left-hand corner of the picture, near the above-mentioned recess, the presentment of a huge human face—not uncomely, with a well-shaped nose, down-turned eyes under strongly marked eyebrows, and a mouth (whether or not shaded by a moustache is uncertain), wearing a smile as inscrutable and enigmatical as that of Mona Lisa.

"Do you suppose that he is dead?" I asked Lord Bute, after studying this strange and sinister countenance for some time in silence.

"No," he replied, in his usual quiet fashion; "he is not dead; but he is saying, 'I know more than you do.'"

I need not say that no one, as far as I know, claims to have ever seen this strange great face actually on the wall, but only on the photograph. Some years ago, Sir Robert Gordon-Gilmour and I visited Liberton House together and closely inspected the scene of the apparition; but we could see nothing except a stretch of dirty and discoloured plaster.

Oddly enough, that is all that many people have been and are able to see, even when carefully examining the photograph here reproduced.

I remember sending the photograph (I think on Bute's advice) to the principal photographic journal for investigation and comment. Its verdict was a very cautious one.

> We cannot be expected, on the evidence before us, to admit that it is really a 'ghost.' But we do not think it in the least probable that the glass had been used before; for no professional photographer would use a glass twice. We believe it would be possible (we cannot say more) to produce a very similar effect by a minute pin-hole in the camera or bellows. We are glad to have had the opportunity of seeing what is, beyond doubt, a distinct curiosity.

This is a fairly non-committal utterance. Personally, I have no belief whatever in the "pin-hole-in-the-camera" theory, which Bute also thought quite untenable.

2. "Cleve Hall"

THIS story the Abbot sent me as well as one which he felt compelled to disguise, writing (23rd June 1937), "as you are interested in such things I send you two more of my ghost articles. The Cleve Hall one has entirely fictitious names and places; but the story is first-hand. Perhaps you recognize the real names. I hope you got my 'Halifax' long article: I fear I have rather damned it with faint praise, though it was fulsomely praised by many Reviewers."

The account of Cleve Hall was as follows:

The high character, deep religious principles, and wide popularity—even with many who did not agree with his ecclesiastical opinions—of the late Lord Halifax, no doubt accounts for the very great interest which has been taken in the collection of ghost stories compiled by him, and brought out by his son since his death.

I have read the book carefully through, and hope to have an opportunity of saying a good deal about it before very long. Meanwhile, as the lengthening evenings of winter are upon us, and the time seems opportune, I want to put on record a very singular story of a haunted house in England which is not mentioned in Lord Halifax's book; though he was well-acquainted with it, and was once at personal pains to try and solve its mystery. My knowledge of every detail is intimate, personal, and first-hand; and as some of the protagonists in the story are still living, I am entirely changing, in telling the tale, the names of both persons and places concerned.

In one of the loveliest English counties, not far from a

famous resort for tourists in quest of health or pleasure, stood, and stands, Cleve Hall, home for many generations of the family of Hall-Selsdon. The most interesting figure of the family in modern times was that of the squire in the latter days of the eighteenth century, who had dangerously meddled with politics in pre-Revolution Paris, had suddenly dropped into an oubliette of the Bastille and vanished from all human ken, so that in due time his brother was allowed to presume his death and take possession of the estate. Then, years later, came the burning of the Bastille, and the release of the prisoners, one of them being the long-lost squire of Cleve. He (so runs the family legend) returned to England and made his way to his old home, where he got but a cold welcome from the brother who had taken his place. In no long time, however, the returned exile disappeared again, this time forever; and the brother remained in possession. It was his grandson, a boy of eighteen, just finishing his course at a Catholic school before going up to the University, who was the young squire of Cleve at the time when I first became acquainted with the family, being then Master of the Ampleforth Hall (now St. Benet's) at Oxford.

In the midsummer of the year I am referring to, the party assembled at Cleve consisted of George Hall-Selsdon, his widowed mother, his brother (a naval cadet at Osborne), his two young sisters, and his maternal uncle, who was spending a holiday with the family. There was a private chapel at Cleve, and a canon from the cathedral town not far distant came every week to say the Sunday Mass. The whole family was enjoying a happy vacation—a long one for George, who was not due to join his college till October.

Near Cleve Hall—indeed in the precincts of the park, was a smaller mansion, or dower-house, which had been empty for some time, but it was now intended to let if possible. It was being done up and renovated; and some pictures and furniture were being removed thither from the Hall, including a rather remarkable portrait; a man in Georgian wig and a blue coat, leaning on a thin sword. It was found in an attic, unframed and dusty, was cleaned and framed and sent to the dower-house with other pictures. The members of the family were interested in it, and had given it the name of the "Man with the Rapier."

The summer days were passing away happily at Cleve, when (I think about mid-August) a feeling began to come over the family, that besides themselves and the domestic staff, there was another presence in the house—at first neither to be seen nor heard, but unmistakably there. Gradually the unknown began to take palpable shape; the place which he haunted being the landing half-way up the stairs. And there most of them, George, his mother, his uncle, and I think the canon (but not the three younger children), saw him time after time, never when they were together, but always when they were alone, ascending or descending the stairs. They saw him always standing, looking as it were out of the window (though that was impossible, for it had within recent years been filled with stained glass): the figure of a man in a white wig and blue coat, leaning on a thin sword. "The Man with the Rapier!" It was only later that they were able to identify the figure as that of the great-uncle who had disappeared, and again so mysteriously disappeared just a hundred years before.

It was George himself who told me that no fear or panic was at any time caused by this Man in Blue, who so strangely materialized at Cleve in those summer evenings. They were all interested in him, and sorry for him, as he stood there, so pale and sad, always looking out of the window through which he could see nothing. The elder members of the family held a council, and agreed that the poor man must want something, and that someone must question him: but who? George's uncle would, and did.

So the uncle dressed early one evening, and came down

half an hour before dinner. There stood the Blue Man on the landing, sad and wan, looking intently at nothing; and there the uncle stood looking at him.

"Tell me," he said gently, "is there anything we can do for you? you look unhappy; can we help you? We will all say our Rosary for you every day for a week; and our chaplain will offer his Mass for you on Sunday."

For the first time the poor ghost turned his head round, looked the uncle in the face, and smiled—a sweet smile which showed pleasure and gratitude and content. The Rosary was duly said, the Mass offered; and once more, once only, the Man in Blue was seen, standing in the old spot. Faint and hardly discernible was his figure; but his features seemed to glow with a supernatural light, and to radiate happiness and peace.

A charming story, is it not? With a happy ending, such as all ghost tales ought to have. Would that this were indeed the end of the hauntings of Cleve Hall! There remains, alas! to be told a tragic and terrible sequel.

Peace now reigned at Cleve Hall. It had never really been disturbed by the unfrightening and rather pathetic apparition of the "Man with the Rapier" to certain members of the Hall-Selsdon family, who were nevertheless relieved that episode was now over, and well over, and their collateral ancestor, as far as they could judge, safe and happy.

But not, I think, later than a week or ten days subsequent to the final appearance of this innocuous ancestor, there came down the Hall a new and alarming sensation—a feeling, nay a certainty, at first unconfessed, but later communicated from one to another, that their home was haunted by another Presence; not gentle and harmless like the poor gentleman in blue, but something menacing and sinister in the highest degree.

"Before we had the slightest inkling as to what it was,"

so George told me, "we all—that is all we elders—felt that there was something in the house which chilled and threatened us. I remember how, morning after morning, we came down to breakfast, generally the cheeriest meal of the day, and sat there mum and depressed, and often in utter silence. We couldn't explain it; but there it was."

And then gradually, as had happened before, the Thing materialized. George, his mother, his uncle, and the chaplain began to perceive, at first very dimly, then with ever-growing distinctness, not on the staircase landing as before, but in their own rooms, a strange and frightening figure, robed in a long grey gown or coat, with a hood over the head, under which appeared a pallid face, with beaked nose, beetling eyebrows, and tight curved lips. Sometimes standing motionless in the corner of the room, sometimes close to the bed, the visitant looked down on the inmate of the room with shiny baleful eyes. Not always motionless, however; it was the canon's evidence, I think, that more than once the unknown had stretched out a claw-like hand and "scrabbled" horribly on the bed-clothes. George himself had at least once had experience of the same phenomenon.

In the midst of these growing alarms, a disquieting event was a letter from the chaplain (an Irishman of the emotional type) to say that he could no longer act as chaplain at Cleve. The Bishop, when appealed to, declined to come himself, as he was invited to do so; but said that he was sending for the weekends an admirable young priest, one Fr. Champ, gifted with piety, courage, and common sense, which would be equal to any emergency that might arise. He duly arrived, and during his weekend sojourn at the hall the nightly apparitions became more insistent and alarming than ever.

One only expedient suggested itself to the harassed family. Someone must, it was clear, summon up courage to accost the unwelcome intruder, and learn, if possible, the reason of his presence.

Once more the intrepid uncle undertook the commission; and on the very next night, seeing the hooded figure standing by his bed, he boldly addressed him, enquiring why he had come to disturb the peace and happiness of this united family, and what reason he could have for making their lives a misery, as he was doing.

The spectre looked down on him, and without apparently moving his lips in speech, replied in four words:

"This is my home."

When George Hall-Selsdon told me this story (it was his first term at Oxford), we were bicycling together on an expedition to Blenheim Palace. So interested was I at this point in the narrative, that we both dismounted from our cycles and stood side by side in the dusty high road.

"George," I said, "on these occasions ghosts very seldom speak. Did your uncle tell you what his voice sounded like when he said those four words?"

"Yes," said George, "he did. He said the sound of the voice was like the feel of a jellyfish."

We rode on in silence.

"Was that all?" I asked at length.

"No," George replied; "my uncle ventured falteringly to suggest, as he had done before, that Rosaries and Masses should be offered for this poor tormented soul. But the only response was a withering look of horror, hate and despair."

All that remained for the haunted family to do was to dispose themselves, as best they could, for the crowning shock of terror which they all felt would surely be encountered at the coming weekend; for it was then, when two Masses were always said in the chapel, that these evil manifestations were ever strongest. So the family disposed itself on the following Saturday to meet the enemy with what courage they could.

The mother took her two youngest daughters to sleep in her own room; the priest retained the usual chaplain's chamber next the chapel; and Vivian (the naval cadet, who had never confessed to having seen or heard anything) remained in his room on the upper floor. The uncle was lodged in the "archroom," so called because an ancient stone arch formed a kind of alcove where the bed was placed; and, finally, George had a low truckle-bed arranged for him in the same room, at the foot of his uncle's bed.

Thus prepared, they said, as always, their Rosary in common, and then retired to rest, knowing not what the night would bring forth.

George was soon in his low couch (his uncle was reading by a bedside lamp) and was—so he told me—just dropping off to sleep, when he was aroused by a sound of scuffling and panting coming from the direction of his uncle's pillow. Silently and slowly he raised his head above the foot of the big four-poster, to see-what? His uncle sitting up in bed swaying to and fro, his wrists clasped in the bony fingers of the Visitor.

No word, only the sound of hard breathing, and desperate struggling. Then George saw the Creature pull his uncle from the bed, and drag his body along the floor till his head knocked with a reverberating thud against one of the stone bases of the pillared arch. Then, George confessed, he lost his head, rushed into the gallery, knocked violently at his mother's door, at Fr. Champ's, even at Vivian's attic upstairs, shouting as he knocked that the Devil had pulled uncle Jack out of bed and was then actually killing him.

But when the roused and panic-stricken family rushed into the arch-room to investigate, they only found Uncle Jack in bed apparently unhurt, though scared and deadly pale.

The chaplain behaved like a trump, and in a minute was in the haunted chamber with purple stole, holy water, and all the paraphernalia of exorcism and devotion. Appropriate prayers were said and the family went back to bed.

But within the week they left their home to the invading demon (if such he was), retired with all possible celerity to the dower-house, and came back to Cleve no more.

Who was the ghostly intruder? Was it the squire who had retained possession of the family seat when his brother reappeared and almost at once disappeared again forever? Who shall say?

3. Lord Bute's Death Warning

ABBOT Sir David Hunter-Blair in his *Memoir of the Marquess of Bute* recalls the ghostly warning heard at Cardiff Castle on the night that his cousin the last Marquess Hastings died. Mr. John Boyle, a Trustee of Lord Bute's father (10th November 1868), "seated in the library, heard a carriage roll through the great courtyard and stop at the door. After an interval, thinking the bell must be broken, he came into the hall, but the butler, who was waiting there, assured him that no carriage had come. He only heard later, for the first time, that the arrival of a spectral carriage was said always to foretell the death of some member of the Hastings family. Mr. Boyle's grandson adds: "My grandfather always told this story very solemnly and with the fullest conviction of its truth though he was not at all apt to believe in anything except the most positive and material facts.'"

Lady Margaret MacRae, Lord Bute's only daughter, assured the Abbot that on the eve of her father's death at Dumfries House (8th October 1900), she was an ear-witness of a precisely similar phenomenon.

XXII: THE SLINDON GHOST

THE old house at Slindon was long a Catholic refuge, being held by the Eyres and the Leslies of Fetternear. The most famous story was Bishop Wilberforce's encounter with the ghost of a priest. Mrs. Morse, *née* Violet Leslie, writes:

The story as I always heard it is as follows. Lady Newburgh had a party, amongst the guests being Bishop Sam Wilberforce. On his way down to dinner he passed a Catholic priest on the stairs. Not seeing him at dinner he asked his neighbour for the reason and who he was, and was told to say nothing about it, as the priest was an apparition and the old lady was nervous. Wilberforce then said that if he had known, he would have spoken to him. Next day, when he was in the library the priest appeared again, so Wilberforce did speak and asked if he could do anything for him. By some means the priest took him to one of the bookcases and made him take down a certain book, open it and remove a paper which was in it. Wilberforce then did not know what to do with it, finally guessing it was the cause of the priest's unrest, he burnt it in the fire and from that moment the priest was never seen again. Wilberforce did not read the paper. I always doubted the truth of the story till one day, when I was grown up, Mrs. Ellicott, widow of the Bishop of Gloucester, came to see us. I had never seen her before and I met her. As she got out of her pony carriage she caught me by the arm and said: "Take me and show me the room where 'Soapy' Sam saw his ghost," which of course I did and asked whatever did she know about it, and she said he had often told her about it. After that I had to believe it.

Stead tells the story badly in one of his volumes and puts the name of the place as Slinfold.

The return of a priest in search of papers is a recurrent

story in the Church, and indeed, if it has occurred once, there is no reason why it should not occur often. For instance, the story Sir Henry Jerningham told of Cossey in Norfolk. He lived there for 25 years with Lord Stafford, who used to see a monk searching in the library amongst the books. Once he sent his chaplain to question the ghost, who told him there was a Confession below the pages of a certain book and that he could not rest until this was destroyed.

XXIII: AUGUSTUS HARE'S GHOST STORIES

A UGUSTUS HARE was a famous writer and collector of ghost stories, some of which had a deep religious flavour. Though they are not always easy to identify, they make wonderful tales. Father Gurdon's ghost story is on a par with the Oratory telephone story. In every country, and perhaps, if truth were told, in every diocese there are such legends, traditions and sometimes evidenced instances. If one soul is divinely permitted to make the sign or gesture necessary to bring a lapsed love or relation back to the Church, it should have occurred hundreds of times. The spiritual economy beyond the veil is not to be estimated. One thing is certain and that is that between the two worlds the Divine Mercy has allowed no Iron Curtain.

Augustus Hare collected his story at Raby Castle (28th October 1887), from "a pleasant Mr. Wilkinson."

1. Father Gurdon's Ghost-Story

ONE day last year, Mr. Gurdon, an excellent Catholic priest belonging to a mission in the East End of London, had come in from his labours dreadfully wet and tired, and rejoicing in the prospect of a quiet evening, when the bell rung, and he was told that a lady wanted to see him on most urgent business. He said to a friend who was with him, how sincerely he dreaded being called out again into the wet that night, and how he hoped that the visit meant nothing of the kind; but he admitted the lady. She was a remarkably sweet, gentle-looking person, who told him that there was a case in most urgent need of his immediate ministrations at No. 24 in a street near, and she implored him to come at once, saying that she would wait to point out the house to him. So he only stayed to change his wet things, and then prepared to follow the lady. He took with him the Host, which he wore against his breast, holding, as is the custom, his hand over it. It is not considered right for a priest carrying the Host to engage in conversation, so Mr. Gurdon did not speak to the lady on the way to the house, but she walked a little way in front of him. At last she stopped, pointed to a house, and said, "This, Father, is No. 24." Then she passed on and left him.

Mr. Gurdon rang the bell, and when the servant came, asked who it was who was seriously ill in the house. The servant looked much surprised and said there was no illness there at all. Much astonished, Mr. Gurdon said he thought the servant must be mistaken, that he had been summoned to the house to a case in most urgent need. The servant insisted that there was no illness; but Mr. Gurdon would not go away without seeing the owner of the house, and was shown up to a sitting-room, where he found the master of the house, a pleasant-looking young man of about five-and-twenty. To him Mr. Gurdon told how he had been brought here, and the young man assured him that there must be some mistake—there was certainly no illness in the house; and to satisfy Mr. Gurdon, he sent down to his servants, and ascertained that they were all perfectly well.

A tea-supper was upon the table, and very cordially and kindly the young man asked Mr. Gurdon to sit down to it with him. He pressed it, so they had tea together and much pleasant conversation. Eventually, the young man said, "I also am a Catholic," adding, in an ingenuous way, "but I fear you would think a very bad one"; and he explained that the sacraments and confession had long been practically unknown to him. "As long as my dear mother lived," he said, "it was different; but she died three years ago, and since her death I have paid no attention to religion." And he described the careless life he had been leading.

Very earnestly and openly Mr. Gurdon talked with him, urging him to amend his ways, to go back to his old serious life. At first he urged it for his mother's sake, then from higher motives. He seemed to make an impression, and the young man was touched by what he said, and said no one had spoken to him thus since his mother died. At last Mr. Gurdon said, "Why should you not begin a new life now? I might hear your confession, and then be able to give you absolution this very evening. But I should not wish you to decide this hurriedly; let me leave you for an hour—let me leave you perfectly alone for that time—you will then be able to think over your confession, and decide what you ought to tell me." The young man consented, but urged Mr. Gurdon not to leave the house again in the rain; there were a fire and lights in the library, would not Mr. Gurdon wait there?

Mr. Gurdon willingly went to spend the time in the library, where two candles were lit on the chimney-piece. Between these he placed the Host. Then he occupied himself with examining the pictures in the room. There were many fine engravings, and there was also a crayon portrait of a lady which struck him very much. He seemed to remember the original quite well, and yet he could not recall where he had seen her. On going back to the other room, he told the young man how very much he had been struck by the picture, "Ah?" he said, "that is the portrait of my dear mother, and it is indeed the greatest comfort I have, it is so very like her." At that moment Mr. Gurdon suddenly recollected where he had seen the lady; she it was who had come to fetch him to the house.

Mr. Gurdon heard the young man's confession and gave him absolution; he seemed to be in the most serious and earnest frame of mind. He could not receive the sacrament, because it must be taken fasting, so the evening meal they had had made it impossible. But it was arranged that he should come to the chapel at eight o'clock the next morning, and that he should receive it then. Mr. Gurdon went home most deeply interested in the case, and truly thankful for having been led to it; but when morning came, and the service took place in the chapel, to his bitter disappointment the young man was not there. He feared that he had relapsed altogether, but he could not leave him thus, and as soon as the service was over he hastened to his house. When he reached it, the blinds were all down. The old female servant who opened the door was in floods of tears; her master had died in his sleep.

On the last evening of his life his mother had brought Mr. Gurdon[11] to him.

2. Count de Fersen and the Cardinal

IN 1874 Hare took down a story from Henry Liddell, 1st Lord Ravensworth, which may be called "Count de Fersen and the Cardinal," for it reveals how the friend of Marie Antoinette was approached by the ghost of a murdered man and by appeal to the Cardinal in charge of the Roman police secured the execution of the murderers. In 1879 Hare repeated the story to the Crown Prince of Sweden who made inquiries as to Count Löwenjelm, Swedish Minister in Rome, and found that facts and dates coincided.

The Count was staying in an inn at Radicofani. He woke in the night and saw in the moonlight the figure of a man dressed in a white cap, jacket, and trousers such as

---

[11] Father Bertie Gurdon was for a time at the London Oratory before taking up work in the East End where he left a church to crown his mission.

masons wear.

Count de Fersen stretched out his hand over the side of the bed to take one of his pistols, and the man said,

"Don't fire: you could do no harm to me, you could do a great deal of harm to yourself: I am come to tell you something."

And the Comte de Fersen looked at him: he did not come any nearer; he remained just where he was, standing in the pool of white moonlight, halfway between the bed and the wall; and he said:

"Say on; tell me what you have come for."

And the figure said,

"I am dead, and my body is underneath your bed. I was a mason of Radicofani, and, as a mason, I wore the white dress in which you now see me. My wife wished to marry somebody else; she wished to marry the landlord of this hotel, and they beguiled me into the inn, and they made me drunk, and they murdered me, and my body is buried beneath where your bed now stands. Now I died with the words vendetta upon my lips and the longing, the thirst that I have for revenge will not let me rest, and I never shall rest, I never can have any rest, till I have had my revenge. Now I know that you are going to Rome; when you get to Rome, go to the Cardinal Commissary of Police, and tell him what you have seen, and he will send men down here to examine the place, my body will be found, and I shall have my revenge."

And the Comte de Fersen said, "I will." But the spirit laughed and said:

"You don't suppose that I'm going to believe that? You don't imagine that you are the only person I've come to like this? I have come to dozens, and they all have said, 'I will,' and afterwards what they have seen has seemed like a hallucination, a dream, a chimæra, and before they have reached Rome the impression has vanished altogether, and nothing has been done. Give me your hand."

The Comte de Fersen was a little staggered at that; however, he was a brave man, and he stretched out his hand over the foot of the bed, and he felt something or other happen to one of his fingers; and he looked, and there was no figure, only the moonlight streaming in through the little latticed window, and the old cracked looking-glass on the wall and the old rickety furniture just distinguishable in the half-light; there was no mason there, but the loud regular sound of the snoring of the courier was heard outside the bedroom door. The Comte de Fersen could not sleep; he watched the white moonlight fade into dawn, and the pale dawn brighten into day, and it seemed to him as if the objects in that room would be branded into his brain, so familiar did they become—the old cracked looking-glass, and the shabby washing-stand, and the rush-bottomed chairs, and he also began to think that what had happened in the earlier part of the night was a hallucination—a mere dream. Then he got up, and began to wash his hands; and on one of his fingers he found a very curious old iron ring, which was certainly not there before—and then he *knew*.

The Comte de Fersen went to Rome, and when he arrived at Rome he went to the Swedish Minister that was then, a certain Count Löwenjelm, and the Count Löwenjelm was very much impressed with the story, but a person who was much more impressed was the Minister's younger brother, the Count Carl Löwenjelm, for he had a very curious and valuable collection of peasants' jewelry, and when he saw the ring he said:

"That is a very remarkable ring, for it is a kind of ring which is only made and worn in one place, and that place is the mountains near Radicofani."

And the two Counts Löwenjelm went with the Comte de Fersen to the Cardinal Commissary of Police, and the Cardinal was also very much struck, and he said:

"It is a very extraordinary story, a very extraordinary

story indeed, and I am quite inclined to believe that it means something, But, as you know, I am in a great position of trust under Government, and I could not send a body of military down to Radicofani upon the faith of what may prove to have been a dream. At any rate (he said) I could not do it unless the Comte de Fersen proved his sense of the importance of such an action by being willing to return to Radicofani himself."

And not only was the Comte de Fersen willing to return, but the Count Carl Löwenjelm went with him. The landlord and landlady were excessively excited when they saw them return with the soldiers who came from Rome. They moved the bed, found that the flags beneath had been recently upturned. They took up the flags, and there—not sufficiently corrupted to be irrecognizable—was the body of the mason, dressed in the white cap and jacket and trousers, as he had appeared to the Comte de Fersen. Then the landlord and landlady, in true Italian fashion, felt that Providence was against them, and they confessed everything. They were taken to Rome, where they were tried and condemned to death, and they were beheaded at the *Bocca della Verita.*

3. The Conversion of Marguerite Pole

ONE of the oldest and most historical of English families is that of the Poles. The last Catholic Archbishop of Canterbury was Cardinal Pole. Extinguished in the main line, they are represented by the Baronetcy of van-Notten-Pole. The third Baronet, Sir Peter (died 1887), married Lady Louisa Pery, daughter of the Earl of Limerick. She appeared to Sir Peter when their beloved daughter Marguerite was making her First Communion as a convert to the Catholic Church. Hare's sister, Esmeralda, was Marguerite's closest friend when they were living in Paris in 1854. Sir Peter had sent for his daughter and informed her: "Esmeralda Hare is about to become a Roman Catholic; now remember that if you ever follow her example, I will turn you out of doors there and then."

Hare comments: "The result of this was that within a week Marguerite Pole had become a Roman Catholic," and he tells the story by quoting some notes of his sister's.

It was Madame Davidoff who led Marguerite Pole across the courtyard of the [Convent of the] *Sacré Cœur* to the little room at the other side of it, where the Père de Ravignan was waiting for her. As she opened the door he looked up in an ecstasy. "*Voilà trois ans*," he said, "*que je prie pour votre arrivée, et vous voila enfin.*"[12] She was quite overcome, and told him that for three years she had seen a figure constantly beckoning her forward, she knew not whither. The Père de Ravignan answered, "I believe that you will see that figure for the last time on the day of your *première communion*", and so it was: the figure stood by her then, and afterwards it disappeared forever.

At first Sir Peter had said that he would turn Marguerite out of doors, and his fury knew no bounds. One evening Marguerite sent her maid privately to me with a note saying, "To-morrow morning I shall declare myself: to-morrow my father will turn me out of doors, and what am I to do?" "Oh," I said, "only have faith and watch what will happen, for it will all come right." And sure enough, so it seemed at the time, for the next morning Sir Peter sent for his housekeeper and said to her, "I've changed my mind. Miss Marguerite shall not go away; and I've changed my mind even so much that I shall send to Mrs. Hare and ask her to take me with her when she goes to see her daughter make her *première communion*."

---

[12] "For three years I have prayed for your arrival, and here you are."

It was quite a great function in the church of the [convent of the] *Sacré Cœur*. I was terrified out of my wits when I saw the crowd in the church, and in the chancel were the Bishop, the Papal Nuncio, and all the principal clergy of Paris, for it was quite an event. Marguerite and I were dressed in white, with white veils and wreaths of white roses. As the Papal Nuncio came forward to place his hands on our heads, in the very act of Confirmation, there was a fearful crash, and Sir Peter fell forward over the bench just behind us, and was carried insensible out of the church. Mamma went with him, for she thought he was dying. When he came to himself his first words were— "Louisa, Louisa! I have seen Louisa." He had seen Lady Louisa Pole.

When Lady Louisa was dying she said to Marguerite:

"My child, there is one thing I regret; it is that I have had doubts about the Roman Catholic Church, and that I have never examined [her claims"].

4. Lord Denbigh's Ghost-Story

IT is often urged that ghosts are not much heard of in Catholic countries compared with the British Isles. This is not so. Perhaps they are less persistent where Masses can be easily procured for their allayance. Hare gives one which he heard from the Earl of Denbigh in 1876. Lord Denbigh had become a Catholic with his wife. His story follows:

Dr. Playfair, physician at Florence, went to the garden of a villa to see some friends of his. Sitting on a seat in the garden, he saw two ladies he knew; between them was a third lady dressed in grey, of very peculiar appearance. Walking round the seat, Dr. Playfair found it very difficult to see her features. In a farther part of the garden he met another man he knew. He stayed behind the seat and asked his friend to walk round and see if he could make out who the odd-looking lady was. When he came back he said, "Of course I could not make her out, because when I came in front of her, her face was turned towards you." Dr. Playfair then walked up to the ladies, and as he did so, the central figure disappeared. The others expressed surprise that Dr. Playfair, having seen them, had not joined them sooner. He asked who the lady was who had been sitting between them. They assured him that there had never been any such person.

The next morning, Dr. Playfair went early to see the old gardener of the villa, and asked him if there was any tradition about the place. He said. "Yes, there is a story of a lady dressed in grey, who appears once in every twenty-five years, and the singular part is that she has no face." Dr. Playfair asked when she had appeared last. "Well, I remember perfectly; it was twenty-five years ago, and the time is about coming round for her to appear again."

These four stories were typical of Augustus Hare's style. For years he had been telling his ghost stories with dramatic gestures in Society and eventually recorded them with their literary embellishment. Under the frills the originals were no doubt based on facts. The stories are taken from *The Story of My Life.*

XXIV: FROM WILLIAM STEAD'S GHOST STORIES

THE late William Stead, editor of the *Review of Reviews*, was a Spiritualist of advanced views. He published a collection of *Real Ghost Stories*[13] which is interesting for the Catholic material. Owing to lapse of time it is impossible to add corroboration or investigation, but they read like the real article and are worth reprinting. The story connected with the Weld family and St. Edmund's College can of course be corroborated.

Mr. Stead kept his busy hands in both worlds. He was anxious to bring about universal Peace by interviewing the heads of State. After interviewing the Czar, he was disappointed not to be allowed an audience with Pope Leo XIII. The truth was, as he was never aware, that he had been reported in Rome as a sorcerer! Rome has perhaps over-estimated the powers of such as Stead and Home by accounting them in the rare class of sorcerers such as Scripture has described for our warning.

1. A Ghost that Wished to Pay Debts

THERE is an odd story told by a Catholic priest in the *Proceedings of the Psychical Society*, which seems to show that considerations of £ s. d. are not altogether forgotten on the other side of the grave. It is as follows:

---

[13] The five following stories are taken from this book.

In July 1838, I left Edinburgh to take charge of the Perthshire missions. On my arrival in Perth I was called upon by a Presbyterian woman, Anne Simpson, who for more than a week had been in the utmost anxiety to see a priest. This woman stated that a woman lately dead (date not given), named Moloy, slightly known to Anne Simpson, had appeared to her during the night for several nights, urging her to go to the priest, who would pay a sum of money, three and tenpence, which the deceased owed to a person not specified.

I made inquiries, and found that a woman of that name had died who had acted as washerwoman and followed the regiment. Following up the inquiry, I found a grocer with whom she had dealt, and on asking him if a female named Moloy owed him anything, he turned up his books and told me that she did owe him three and tenpence. I paid the sum. Subsequently the Presbyterian woman came to me, saying that she was no more troubled.

2. A Priest's Vision

I AM a "Popish" priest stationed in a country district, lead a very quiet life, and am free from excitements of any kind. I enjoy excellent health and I am thankful to say, possess a sound mind in a sound body. I am by no means superstitious; and my friends describe me as a most unimpressionable man. On the afternoon of Wednesday, the 30th of September of this present year, I visited one of my sick people, a man who had been suffering from a chest disease for many years. I heard his confession, and having chatted with him for some time, left the house, promising to bring him Holy Communion the following morning. I walked briskly home, a distance of about two miles or thereabouts, calling at one house on the way. I reached my cottage shortly before dusk, and while my servant was preparing my tea I amused myself by glancing over the paper which had arrived by the afternoon post. While I was folding over the sheet I happened to look across the room. I was simply astounded at what I saw. It seemed as if the opposite wall had disappeared. I distinctly saw poor John's (the sick man I had visited that afternoon) bed. There was the man himself, so it seemed to me, sitting up in the bed and looking straight at me. I saw him as distinctly as I now see this paper upon which I write. I was greatly astonished, but by no means frightened. I sat staring at the appearance for quite five seconds, and then it gradually disappeared in much the same fashion as a "dissolving view," the wall coming back again to sight as the other picture faded away. At first I thought that it had no objective reality, but was purely subjective. But then John and his illness were not at all in my mind. I was thinking about what I was reading. I had often visited this particular man, had seen many sick people, and had been present at the death of several; besides, I did not think that John was, as yet, near death.

The next morning, as I was entering the church, to say Mass, I saw John's wife in the porch, crying, "O Father!" she cried out, "my heart is broken. O Father! John, my dear one, died last night, and so sudden! You hadn't gone an hour scarce. He (John) sits up in the bed and he says:

"'Is the Father gone, Moll?'

"'Why?' says I, 'didn't you say good-bye to he, Jack?'

"'Ah, yes,' says he, 'but I wants he. I'm bad, Moll. I'm a dyin', he's to say Mass for me, mind that'; and with your name on his lips, father, he fell back-dead."

I ascertained that it was heart disease.

I did not mention what I saw to the woman, nor have I mentioned it to a single soul, except to yourself. If it got known that I had seen a spirit in my house it would be all over with my comfort. My housekeeper would pack off, and I should be left to make my own bed, scrub my own house down, and cook my own food. You must, therefore, accept my statement for what it is worth in your own estimation. I can only give you my bare word that it is quite true, that I have no wish to deceive, and that, as a priest of God's true Church, I should not so far forget my mission as to propagate a falsehood.

3. Doubles Summon a Priest to their Deathbeds

THE narrative rests on the excellent authority of the Rev. Father Fleming, the hard-working Catholic priest of Slindon, in Sussex. I heard it from one of his parishioners who is a friend of mine, and on applying to Father Fleming he was kind enough to write out the following account of his strange experience, for the truth of every word of which he is prepared to vouch. In all the wide range of spectral literature I know no story that is quite like this:

I was spending my usual vacation in Dublin in the year 1868, I may add very pleasantly, since I was staying at the house of an old friend of my father's, and whilst there was treated with the attention which is claimed by an honoured guest, and with as much kindness and heartiness as if I were a member of the family. I was perfectly comfortable, perfectly at home. As to my professional engagements, I was free for the whole time of my holiday, and could not in any manner admit a scruple or doubt as to the manner in which my work was done in my absence, for a fully qualified and earnest clergyman was supplying for me. Perhaps this preamble is necessary to show that my mind was at rest, and that nothing in the ordinary course of events would have recalled me so suddenly and abruptly to the scene of my labours at Woolwich. I had about a week of my unexpired leave of absence yet to run when what I am about to relate occurred to me. No comment or explanation is offered. It is simply a narrative.

I had retired to rest at night, my mind perfectly at rest, and slept, as young men do in robust health, until about four o'clock in the morning. It appeared to me about that hour that I was conscious of a knock at the door. Thinking it to be the manservant, who was accustomed to call me in the morning, I at once said, "Come in." To my surprise there appeared at the foot of the bed two figures, one a man of medium height, fair and well-fleshed, the other tall, dark and spare, both dressed as artisans belonging to Woolwich Arsenal. On asking them what they wanted, the shorter man replied, "My name is C—— . I belong to Woolwich. I died on——of——and you must attend me."

Probably the novelty of the situation and feelings attendant upon it, prevented me from noticing that he had used the past tense. The reply which I received to my question from the other man was like in form, "My name is M——. I belong to Woolwich. I died on——of——and you must attend me." I then remarked that the past tense had been used and cried out, "Stop! You said *died* and the day you mentioned has not come yet!" at which they both smiled and added, "We know this very well; it was done to fix your attention, but" —and they seemed to say very earnestly and in a marked manner—"you must attend us!" at which they disappeared, leaving me awe-stricken, surprised and thoroughly aroused from sleep. Whether what I narrate was seen during sleep or when wholly awake, I do not pretend to say. It appeared to me that I was perfectly awake and perfectly conscious. Of this I had no doubt at the time, and I can scarcely summon up a doubt as to what I heard and saw whilst I am telling it. As I had lighted my lamp, I rose, dressed and seating myself at a table in the room, read and thought and I need hardly say, from time to time prayed fervently, until day came. When I was called in the morning, I sent a message to the lady of the house to say that I should not go to the University

Chapel to say Mass that morning and should be present at the usual family breakfast at nine.

On entering the dining-room, my hostess very kindly inquired after my health, naturally surmising that I had omitted Mass from illness or at least want and consequent indisposition. I merely answered that I had not slept well— that there was something weighing heavily on my mind which obliged me to return at once to Woolwich. After the usual regrets and leave-takings, I started by the midday boat for England. As the first date mentioned by my visitors gave me time, I travelled by easy stages, and spent more than two days on the road, although I could not remain in Dublin after I had received what appeared to me then, and appears to me still, as a solemn warning.

On my arrival at Woolwich, as may be easily imagined, my brother clergy were very puzzled at my sudden and unlooked-for return, and concluded that I had lost my reckoning, thinking that I had to resume my duties a week earlier than I was expected to do. The other assistant priest was waiting for my return to start on his vacation—and he did so the very evening of my return. Scarcely, however, had he left the town when the first of my visitors sent in a request for me to go at once to attend him. You may, perhaps, imagine my feelings at that moment. I am sure you cannot realize them as I do even now after the lapse of so many years. Well, I lost no time. I had, in truth, been prepared, except hat and umbrella, from the first hour after my return. I went to consult the books in which all the sick-calls were entered and to speak to our aged, respected sacristan who kept them. He remarked at once, "You do not know this man, Father; his children come to our school, but he is, or always has been, considered as a Protestant." Expressing my surprise, less at the fact than at his statement, I hurried to the bedside of the sufferer. After the first few words of introduction were over he said, "I sent for you, Father, on Friday morning early, and they told me that you were away from home, but that you were expected back in a few days, and I said I would wait." I found the sick man had been stricken down by inflammation of the lungs, and that the doctor gave no hope of his recovery, yet that he would probably linger some days. I applied myself very earnestly indeed to prepare the poor man for death. Again the next day, and every day until he departed this life, did I visit him, and spent not minutes, but hours, by his bedside.

A few days after the first summons came the second. The man had previously been a stranger to me, but I recognized him by his name and appearance. As I sat by his bedside he told me, as the former had already done, that he had sent for me, had been told that I was absent, and had declared that he would wait for me. Thus far their cases were alike. In each case there was a great wrong to be undone, a conscience to be set right that had erred and erred deeply—and not merely that, it is probable, from the circumstances of their lives, that it was necessary that their spiritual adviser should have been solemnly warned. They made their peace with God, and I have seldom assisted at a deathbed and felt greater consolation than I did in each and both of these. Even now, after the lapse of many years, I cannot help feeling that I received a very solemn warning in Dublin, and am not far wrong in calling it, the Shadow of Death.

4. The Patron Saint of the Welds

ONE of the best-authenticated ghosts on record is that of Philip Weld, who appeared to his father after he had been drowned, accompanied by two persons, one of whom was never recognized and the third was subsequently discovered to be St. Stanislaus Kostka. Philip Weld had been drowned when at St. Edmund's College in

Hertfordshire. The Principal went to Southampton next day to break the news to the boy's father. He met Mr. Weld walking towards Southampton. He immediately stopped the carriage, alighted, and was about to address him when Mr. Weld prevented him by saying:

"You need not say one word, for I know that Philip is dead. Yesterday afternoon I was walking with my daughter, Katherine, and we suddenly saw him. He was standing on the path, on the opposite side of the turnpike road, between two persons, one of whom was a youth dressed in a black robe.

This is a story which can be verified. From St. Edmund's College, Fr Nicholas Kelly writes (19th January 1950):

I am sending you the correct version of the Weld ghost story. The first part, which concerns the accident itself, is substantially the same as given in Mgr. Ward's History of St. Edmund's College. It is based on the testimony of Rev. Henry Telford set down in a letter written from Newton Hall, Blackrock (July 13, 1891). He was Prefect here at the time of the accident. The story of Philip's apparition is told in the words of his sister. I enclose a copy of it written many years ago.

Philip Weld, brother of Monsignor Weld, of Isleworth, and nephew to the Cardinal of that name who died in 1837, was the youngest son of Mr. James Weld, of Archer's Lodge, Southampton. He came to St. Edmund's in 1841, and from the first was a well-conducted and amiable boy, much loved by his companions and superiors. He had been at the College nearly five years when he met with his death, under the following circumstances:

The accident occurred on the Thursday in Easter week, 1846. On that day Philip asked leave for some six or seven lay students to go to Hertford. The leave was granted, and it was arranged that the dinner for the party should, for their accommodation, be ordered for four o'clock on their return. They left the College at ten o'clock. Hertford lies about seven miles south-west of Old Hall. Ten miles direct south from the College, on the east bank of the Lea, stands the Rye House, scene of the plot against the Royal brothers, Charles II and James Duke of York. The students had secretly induced the master, to whose care they were confided, to take them to the Rye House instead of Hertford. Without the knowledge of the superiors they had arranged that a conveyance should be waiting for them on the road. They took their seats in high spirits, with fine weather, and a day of pleasure before them. They reached their destination soon after eleven, and a very few minutes later were enjoying their sport on the River Lea.

All went well till the afternoon, when the time came for setting out homewards. It was nearly three o'clock and Philip petitioned for one more row. Leave for this being granted, they went some little way up the river, but when they finally turned back, through an unlooked-for movement of the boat, Philip was thrown out into the river. The water only reached up to his waist, and no immediate danger was apprehended. Joseph Barron, who was one of the party, offered to reach him an oar, but he refused it, saying, "Row the boat over me." These were his last words for he immediately sank and never rose again. It was afterwards found that when he had fallen from the boat he had alighted on the verge of a deep layer of clay at the bottom of the river, which, yielding under his weight, held his feet in the tenacious soil, and he lay stretched at the bottom of the river beneath the bank. Drags were procured, from the Rye House, but they failed to grapple the body as it lay in its protected position.

The master sent the students home immediately, and directed Joseph Barron to announce the painful fact to the President, Dr. Cox, whilst he remained to superintend the endeavours to raise the body. The President hastened to the riverside and remained there till nightfall, but had to return to the College while the body remained beneath the water. Next morning, he repaired early to the scene, and had the satisfaction of finding that the body had been recovered. The Master of Enfield Lock had lowered the river; the movement of the water had shifted the body and placed it where the drags were able to grapple it, and they drew it to the surface.

Dr. Cox did not return to the College that day, but proceeded by train to London and thence to Southampton, to break the news to Philip's father. On his arrival, he went first to the priest, the Rev. Joseph Siddons. When he had told him what had occurred, they both drove to Archer's Lodge to inform Mr. Weld, Father Siddons undertaking to act as spokesman.

Before they reached the entrance to the grounds, they met Mr. Weld walking towards the town, according to his custom at that time of day. Dr. Cox immediately stopped the carriage, and Fr. Siddons began thus:

"It has seemed good to Almighty God, Mr. Weld, to call your son to Himself by the same element which first conveyed to him Grace." Mr. Weld's answer took them both by surprise, and as it contained his account of the apparition of his son, it shall be given as Miss Weld describes it. According to her he spoke as follows:

"You need not say one word, for I know that Philip is dead. Yesterday afternoon I was walking with my daughter Katherine, and we suddenly saw him. He was standing on the path, at the opposite side of the turnpike road, between two persons, one of whom was a youth dressed in a black robe. My daughter was the first to perceive them, and exclaimed, 'Oh; papa, did you ever see anything so like Philip as that is? 'Like him,' I answered, 'Why it is him!'

"Strange to say my daughter thought nothing of the circumstance, beyond that we had seen an extraordinary likeness of her brother. We walked on towards these three figures. Philip was looking with a smiling happy expression of countenance at the young man in a black robe, who was shorter than himself. Suddenly they all seemed to me to have vanished. I saw nothing but a countryman whom I had seen before. I however said nothing to anyone, as I was fearful of alarming my wife. I looked out anxiously for the post the following morning—to my delight no letter came. I forgot that letters from Ware came in the afternoon, and my fears were quieted, and I thought no more of the extraordinary circumstance until I saw you in the carriage outside my gate. Then, everything returned to my mind, and I could not feel a doubt but that you came to tell me of the death of my dear boy."

The reader may imagine how inexpressibly astonished Dr. Cox was at these words. He asked Mr. Weld if he had ever before seen the young man in the black robe, at whom Philip was looking with such a happy smile. He answered that he had never before seen him, but that his countenance was so indelibly impressed on his mind that he was certain he should know him at once anywhere. Dr. Cox then related to the afflicted father all the circumstances of his son's death, which had taken place at the very hour in which he appeared to his father and sister, and they concluded that he had died in the Grace of God and was in happiness because of the placid smile on his face. Mr. Weld thanked God most fervently for granting him the consolation in his bitter trial.

When Mr. Weld left the church after the funeral of his son, he looked round in passing out to see if any of them resembled the young man he had seen with him, but he could not trace the slightest likeness in anyone amongst them.

About four months after, he and his family were on a visit to his brother Mr. George Weld, at Seagrave Hall, in Lancashire. He went with his daughter Katherine to the neighbouring village of Chipping, and after attending a service at the church, called on the priest, the Rev. Father

Raby (I think). They waited in the parlour for some little time before the priest came, and they amused themselves by looking at the framed prints on the wall. Suddenly Mr. Weld stopped before a picture which had no name written under it that you could see (as the frame covered it) and exclaimed:

"*That* is the person whom I saw with Philip. I do not know whose likeness it is supposed to be, but I am *certain* that *that* is the person whom I saw with Philip."

The priest entered the room a few moments after, and was immediately questioned about the print. He answered that it was a likeness to St. Stanislaus Kostka. Mr. Weld was much moved when he heard this, for St. Stanislaus was a Jesuit who died when quite young; and Mr. Weld's father having been a great benefactor to that Order, his family were supposed to be under the particular protection of the Jesuit Saints. Also Philip had been led of late by various circumstances to special devotion to St Stanislaus. Moreover, St. Stanislaus is supposed to be the special advocate of drowned men, as is mentioned in his life. Father Raby presented the picture to Mr. Weld, who of course received it with the greatest veneration, and kept it until his death. His wife valued it equally and at her death it passed into the possession of the daughter who saw the apparition with him, and she has it now in her possession.

Philip Weld's body was buried in the Sanctuary of the Old Chapel but was transferred to the vaults under the Sanctuary of the New Chapel when it was opened in 1883. A brass plate on the wall of the Chapel cloister records the accident. It bears this inscription:

"Pray for the soul of Philip Weld who was accidentally drowned on 16th day of April, 1846, aged 17 years.

"Jesus, mercy. Ladye, help."

5. Three Unverified Stories

THE Catholic Church abounds in ghost stories in which the ghost has a practical object for revisiting the world. Father Keating, S.J., told me last September that when he was at the College of the Propaganda at Rome, a Danish student died. He had been in the habit of writing out his confessions before he went to the confessional. A short while after the student's death his confessor heard a knock at the door. He said, "Come in." The door opened, and the young Danish student entered the room. Although the priest knew he was dead, he was not frightened, and asked him what he wanted.

He said, "Will you look in my Latin dictionary? You will find there a paper on which I wrote down my last confession which I wished to make to you, but I was taken off before I saw you."

The priest asked him if he was happy.

"Yes," said he, "quite happy. That confession is the only thing that is troubling me. Will you get it?" The priest said he would, and the interview ended.

He then went to the dictionary, and there, between the pages, he found the written confession. He read it, and then destroyed it. The young student never afterwards appeared.

I hope to get confirmation of this from Rome, but as yet I have not received any reply to my inquiries, the person concerned being absent on his travels.

Father Keating also told me a story of a priest whom he said he knew, who had entered the priesthood because of a ghost which appeared to him in an old country house. He followed this ghost to the room which it haunted. It pointed to a place in the floor and disappeared; they took up the floor, and found the sacred vessels which had been hidden these since the time of the Reformation, and which still contained some of the Host or sacred wafer. The vessels were removed and the ghost ceased to haunt. This story also needs verification, and until it is forthcoming it cannot be regarded as having any evidential value.

Another Catholic legend is the familiar story of the persistent haunting of the library at Slindon, Arundel, by the ghost of a Catholic priest. The story goes that he had forgotten to destroy the confession of a penitent. He had placed it between the leaves of the book he was reading. Sudden death deprived him of the opportunity of destroying the paper, and he was unable to rest in his grave until he found it and got someone to destroy it. Every night he revisited the library and hunted for the confession. At last a Catholic priest saw him and asked him what was the matter. He told him eagerly, and pointed out the book, in which the confession was found. He destroyed it at once, and the grateful spirit disappeared. Such is the local tradition, which, however, has never been verified so far as I can discover, but the same story is told of a library near Paris, where, oddly enough, Bishop Wilberforce is said to have been the liberating agent.[14]

---

[14] A slight mistake here. It was always the Slindon apparition that Bishop Wilberforce was connected.

XXV: THE COMPACT AFTER DEATH

ALL through ghostly history, far back into the past comes the story of the soul which was allowed to return to fulfill a compact and to assure some beloved one left on earth. Shakespeare was not speaking sooth in certain famous lines of *Hamlet,* for some spirits, perhaps many, have appeared from that distant bourne whence no traveller is said to return. The reason is often a religious one: to assure the living that the dead have survived. Sometimes it carries a doctrinal complexion: for instance the most famous of the kind known as "The Beresford Ghost Story" told with perfection by Eleanor Alexander (daughter of the Irish Primate) in *Lady Anne's Walk.* Lord Halifax had the story from a roundabout source and all versions differ. Lord Halifax calls it "The Death of Lord Tyrone" and makes the mistake of thinking the hero and heroine were brother and sister.

During the eighteenth century, Deism was prevalent in the ruling classes of Ireland. Deism was the religion of the Freemasons, accepting the Deity without any revelation. Lord Tyrone and the future Lady Beresford, then Nicola Hamilton, were brought up in Deism. The time came when they wavered between Deism and Christian revelation and they promised each other that whichever died first should return and assure the other of the truth beyond the grave. In due time Lord Tyrone's ghost appeared unexpectedly, announced his death and assured Lady Beresford of the truth of revealed religion. Her doubts he scattered by touching her wrist and withering her sinews, over which she wore a black ribbon till the hour of her own death.

Her children removed the ribbon before her burial and gazed at a shrivelled wrist. Her portrait at Tyrone House in Dublin used to show the black ribbon, but the portrait is not at the family seat at Curraghmore. The story spread like wildfire and was copied into the family dossiers of Irish families. If it were true, it offered a proof of revealed religion more striking than all the evidential buttresses erected by Archdeacon Paley. It has reached literary shape, but it is only the central incident for which the reader craves proof. If it was only piously imagined, it must be granted to have had effects. Deism died out of the Irish aristocracy who betook themselves later to all that was Evangelical.

Divine interest in the Beresford family was further shewn when Nicola Beresford's great-great-grandson became Archbishop of Armagh and Primate of All-Ireland.

This ghost story has been as often contested as it has been related. Naturally it has not been popular with Deists or Unitarians, whose principal tenet it destroys. The famous picture with its secondary proof cannot be found but recently I found mention in an old time Diary of a relic which bore physical traces of the strange event. Even this had been removed but what follows is the only record of the locality of the ghostly appearance I have ever found. It occurs in the MS. Diary of Mr. J. I. Burges of Parkanaur, Co. Tyrone (16th July 1863):

We drove to Gill Hall, the residence of the Magills and now of Lord Clanwilliam. The house was built in the time of William III. There is a good Hall and dining room and old-fashioned staircase and a gallery room on the first landing. In a bed-chamber off this apartment the ghost of Lord Tyrone appeared to Lady Beresford and a small cabinet is shewn with a mark upon it, but it is not the real one which it is said was removed by Lady Clanwilliam's grandmother years ago.

Strangely, I have recently been shewn the actual strip of black ribbon which was worn by Lady Beresford over her withered wrist until the hour of her death. It has been carefully preserved as an heirloom in a line of descent.

This compact to appear after death has occurred in the Catholic family of De Salis.

I found an account at Parham Park in Sussex in a MS. book; which Mr. Clive Pearson permitted me to examine, entitled *Cursoni opera*. The story was copied from a manuscript lent by the Duke of Somerset in May 1836 to the former owners of Parham, who were Curzons. The story told how a Countess de Salis had wished to marry her cousin William, but was prevented by her mother. He had asked her to promise that whichever died first should appear to the other; and this she faithfully promised. She was then married to the Count de Salis. William had set out for Ireland to challenge the Count but to his despair he arrived too late. She refused to let him even see her again, so he entered the Army in Spain. Two years later she awoke and saw him standing at her bedside. She cried out with surprise, but he bade her touch the heart which once beat for her. It was a dreadful sensation, like melting ice, and the figure then disappeared. The Count permitted her to wear mourning as though for a sister. She learnt later that he had died of his wounds. Years later her own sister reminded her of the promise she had made with the dead man. The sister had overheard their conversation and remembered the compact which the Countess de Salis forgot.

Lord Brougham, Chancellor of England, made a compact with a College friend of the same nature. To his astonishment his friend, who had died in the Indian Civil Service, appeared to him while he was taking a warm bath, and the great master of evidence noted the date 19th December 1799. A letter arrived later certifying his friend's death on that day. This is recorded in his Memoirs.

A story told me at Stonyhurst concerns a Canon who at Harrow made compact with a College friend that whichever died first the other should say Mass on the anniversary. The Canon did so on behalf of his friend, but the first time he had forgotten, he heard a voice saying to him on the vigil of the date that he wanted the Mass said. After a few more years had lapsed he forgot again. This time his dead friend actually appeared. He went to Cardinal Bourne who told him to say fifty Masses and then omit the Anniversary. He did so and had no more trouble.

XXVI: A DIABOLIC INTERVENTION

THE following story is interesting in that the chief events described are of recent date, and are fully documented with statements made at the time by many of the witnesses who underwent various experiences. Moreover, at least in the earlier stages of the alleged manifestations, individual witnesses were unaware that others had previously seen, heard, or felt anything untoward. The case is unsatisfying in that any attempt to explain it in "scientific"' terms, to suggest the cause or purpose of the manifestations, or to draw a moral from them seems impossible. The refusal of most of the participants to allow their identity to be disclosed and the legal obligation of concealing that of the property affected enforces the strictest anonymity. At the same time, the present writer has had the opportunity not only of reading the official dossier of the case, which comprises documents covering a period of over two years, but of cross-questioning a number of the witnesses to what seems to have been an authentic intervention in human affairs by a spirit, and an evil one at that.

The scene is a house in the English countryside, a rather large house according to modern ideas, standing in its own grounds, with over a dozen bedrooms. It presents anything but that aspect of mystery and gloom traditionally associated with ghost stories. Built on mediæval foundations with traces of Tudor architecture in the cellars, the greater part of the house, added by the succeeding generations, is Georgian in style, with large windows, light, airy rooms, wide passages with no dark corners, and is lit abundantly with electricity. The garden is large and modern with flower beds and lawns, in one of which, somewhat over-close to the house, there is a small but deep pond, presumably fed by underground springs. This is believed to be an old quarry, the stone from which may have been used for building the original house. It features later in the tale, though the earlier manifestations seemed at the time to have no connection with it.

At the date the story begins, a newly married couple, both Catholics, owned the house which had been in continuous occupation previous to their purchase. They had lived in it happily for about ten years. No rumour was heard in the countryside that there was anything queer about the house, nor is that part of England greatly given to stories of ghosts, bogles, pixies or things of that type. One day, in midsummer, a young man staying in the house called on a local doctor, asking for a full medical examination. As both his appearance and the necessary tests showed him to be in bounding health, the doctor asked bluntly for an explanation. This was given, and, after promises of professional secrecy, put into writing then and there. It appears that on a sunny June day, just after lunch, the young man and the lady of the house were walking through a room leading by French windows to the lawn, when the young man suddenly fainted. There was a commotion. When he came to, he let it be understood that his heart might be slightly strained. This explanation was accepted on his promise to go and see a doctor at once. The truth was quite otherwise. He said that on glancing back over his shoulder as he followed his hostess out of the house, he had seen close behind him a figure with its hands covering its face. Since he was of a decidedly husky masculine type, the doctor, who knew him well, suggested this was insufficient reason for his patient's faint. The young man agreed, saying that really why he had fainted was a strong intuition that should the figure withdraw its hands and disclose its face he would inevitably die of shock. No hint of this unpleasant event was given at the time to anyone apart from the doctor who took down the statement.

One evening while it was still broad daylight about two months later, a housemaid, going about her legitimate business in a room—actually the same one in which the young man had had his experience and fainted—was surprised to see by the window opposite a figure which for a moment she took to be that of the owner of the house whom she had just seen elsewhere. On the instant she recognized this figure to be that of a stranger, it seemed to her to move slowly through a solid wall and disappear. Being a woman of considerable courage and character, she said nothing to anyone at the time, but told her doctor whom she visited next day, and who happened to be the same doctor to whom the young man had previously related the story told above. Under a similar pledge of professional secrecy, the housemaid also agreed to make a written declaration, which included a detailed description of the figure, as did the story of the young man. The two descriptions tally, though the housemaid felt no undue sense of fear since, to use her owns words, "it did not seem as though the figure was interested in me."

The figure seen by the young man and the housemaid in broad daylight was opaque in the sense that light did not pass through it. Nevertheless, it did not give a three-dimensional impression; while its outline was curiously vague. Both witnesses saw the figure for a few seconds only, but under cross-questioning proved to be excellent observers. The figure seemed to be draped or composed of a dirty brown substance —if "substance" is the right word to use. It cast no shadow nor were any feet visible. When it moved, the figure seemed to ripple or undulate in a manner difficult to describe, as though the undulations took place in the substance itself. Neither observer saw a face, but the clear suggestion of hands described by the young man as covering the face showed them to be apparently of the same substance as the rest of the figure or its other coverings or draperies, or whatever word can best describe the apparent surface seen. The figure was somewhat less than the medium height of a man and gave a squat and ungainly impression. In both cases it seemed to be hunch-backed or hunched up, whether still or in movement.

These are the only two occasions during the whole two years and more on which this, or for that matter any, figure was seen by anyone. On the other hand, from that time onwards various other curious events took place in the house with increasing frequency. For example, a priest staying in the house was awakened by heavy knocks on his bedroom door. He turned on the light, sat up in bed and said, "Come in." The door did not open, but, as the priest put in the written declaration which he himself drew up a few days later, something did come in, accompanied by a sense of abject terror. This something was invisible but not inaudible. For two hours it was as though a large animal perambulated the room, grunting and gasping, paying no attention to the Reverend Father's adjurations to depart. The priest said nothing to the owners of the house at the time.

Again, an army officer visiting the house for a weekend and who incidentally was not sleeping in the room previously occupied by the priest, was found to have departed before breakfast on Sunday morning, leaving a lame note of excuse and apology for his host. On being asked by a mutual friend a day or two later why he had behaved so strangely, the army officer told in confidence an extraordinary story. This too was committed to paper. It appeared that on going to bed on the Saturday evening at about half past eleven, he had just turned out his bedside lamp when he suddenly felt fingers stroke his face. He naturally turned on the lamp again at once but nothing was to be seen. Thinking he must have been the victim of delusion, he turned out the lamp once more when immediately the same thing happened. Yet a third time, fingers touched his face soon after the light was extinguished. This was unpleasant but the officer declared he was only a little disturbed and in no sense terrified. He got up, searched the room after turning on all the lights, and, feeling anything but sleepy, began to read a book in bed. He soon found he could not concentrate on what he was reading; terrible ideas, wholly foreign to his nature, pressed in upon him. These gradually developed into an urge to kill himself for no logical reason save a black wall of hopeless despair. For an hour or more he fought this notion with his common sense. There was nothing in his normal life or mind even faintly justifying so dreadful and desperate an act, but the idea grew like a fog thickening. There came a desire that he should go and drown himself in the pond outside the house, which up to that moment he had hardly noticed. This officer states that at one moment he found himself actually climbing out of the bedroom window. Suddenly all pressure was removed, leaving the unfortunate victim so weak and shaken that he felt he could not face remaining in the house.

On another occasion, the lady of the house and a woman friend were going upstairs to bed having turned out the lights on the bottom floor. The stairs themselves were brilliantly lit and yet both women heard heavy footsteps coming up behind them, which they described as like those of a man wearing carpet slippers soaked in water. While they shrank against the wall, the footsteps passed up the stairs beside them and disappeared down a lighted corridor. Nothing was seen. This event, which took place some twelve months after the figure had twice been seen in daylight, made it no longer possible, or even desirable, to maintain secrecy. The owner of the house, who had himself experienced nothing and heard no stories of alleged mysterious happenings in his house up to that time, sought the counsel of two friends, one of whom happened to be the doctor who had been consulted by the two witnesses of the brown hunchbacked figure. Permission was obtained to disclose their stories, and by one means and another there came to light not only the experience of the priest and the army officer described above, but a number of others which different persons associated with the house had undergone at various times during the previous months.

Amongst other experiences described was that of a visitor who had slept in yet a different room, and who, like the priest, had been woken up by a heavy rapping on his door. He did not bid the visitor come in but switched on his bedside light, and was astonished to see "the hearthrug fly up the chimney." This somewhat ludicrous performance lost its humour when the bewildered observer remembered clearly that the fireplace had no hearthrug. He got up, opened the door and found nothing in the passage. He then examined the chimney, which was painted white, and having assured himself that no sort of optical illusion would account for what he had seen, he noticed that the register was already in place and the chimney thus completely closed. He is firm in putting down his terrifying nightmare when he got to sleep again after making a careful note of the affair, to ordinary reaction from his disturbing experience. This may have been so, but it is interesting that the vague recollection of his dream in the morning showed it to have been connected with drowning, hatred and horror.

Several people made declarations of being woken up in the night by knockings and one other daylight experience was recorded, though this took place after the private inquiry into the business had been set on foot. The owner of the house, having up to that date experienced absolutely nothing unusual, was engaged one morning hammering a large nail into the wall of the staircase for the purpose of hanging there a big family portrait. He had ascended a few steps of a solid, new and firm stepladder, set squarely on a broad flat landing. A friend standing below had his hand lightly resting on the stepladder and was looking at the hammering operation taking place only some four feet above his head. The friend was startled to see the owner of the house apparently throw the hammer violently back over his shoulder and make a decidedly athletic and dangerous backwards leap from the steps to the stairs. Beyond a slight vibration inseparable from an exercise of this type, the stepladder did not budge and the friend, after ensuring that the owner of the house was unhurt, not unnaturally asked him what he thought he was playing at. The latter said that just as he was about to hit the nail with the hammer for the first time while holding the six-inch wire nail in his left hand, he felt the hammer wrenched out of his right hand by some terrific force. His subsequent jump had been purely instinctive.

There is no need in this account of apparent hauntings to catalogue the many varied and odd experiences which came to light during the inquiry, some of which duplicate the experiences of others, while some were rejected as of doubtful accuracy or authenticity. One other story must however be told. Although it was not recorded at the time, it was recollected that about three months before the first appearance of the figure, a child sleeping in the house kept on having bad dreams which were foreign to its nature, and complained to its mother that "mice" ran over its face after it was dark. There were no mice in the room the child occupied, though traps were set as an assurance. When the child was moved to a room in a different part of the house both dreams and "mice" ceased. This recollection is of particular interest in connection with the later recorded story of the army officer who felt fingers stroke his cheek in the dark, and also in that the particular room of which the child complained had not previously been slept in. Research showed that for at least thirty years, and probably longer, it had been used only as a storeroom.

Once all these stories were put together and examined a few possibly significant facts seemed to emerge. No trace existed in living memory of anything untoward prior to the bad dreams and "mice" of the child, after which the inexplicable events had taken place with increasing frequency. In so far as concerned manifestations at night, it was at once apparent that, wherever the time had been recorded by the witness it was always almost exactly two o'clock in the morning. So far as could be ascertained the same hour fitted the experiences of others who had not thought to look at a clock. Again, no manifestation was recorded or reported by night or day save on one or two days either side of a full moon, though what such a terrestrial event could have to do with apparently spiritual disturbances was clear to no one at the time. However, the priest who eventually exorcised the ghost, as recorded below, said that he had once come across a similar phenomenon and was impressed by the coincidence.

Despite the varied nature of the manifestations, it was found that all had taken place in only one part of the house, curiously enough the newest, where every room, with one possible exception, the staircase and all passages were connected with at least one sinister event: the smaller part where were located the kitchens, offices and bedrooms used by the servants, with one or two spare rooms, had nothing recorded against them. The possible connection was noted between the child's tale of mice and fingers stroking a face in the dark, together with the impressed ideas of suicide, wet feet and despair, for there were stories of dreams and depressions available other than those recorded here.

This inquiry, which was kept as confidential as possible

and of which for practical reasons the servants in the house learned nothing, with the exception of the maid who had seen the figure some eighteen months earlier but had had no other unpleasant experience, was interrupted by a terrible event. One afternoon another maid quietly put down her dustpan and brush, walked straight out of the house and jumped into the pond on the lawn. She was dead when her body was recovered. The subsequent inquest, both official and unofficial, disclosed no sort of reason why this poor woman should have committed suicide. Her life contained no apparent sorrow or dread secret, and though the official verdict of suicide while the balance of her mind was upset received some support from vague stories of a far-off relation in a Home for the feeble-minded, private inquiry never identified the latter.

This sad occurrence naturally caused talk in the village, but without producing any stories of ghosts or hauntings. At the same time an elderly and taciturn farmer of the neighbourhood, whose grandfather had been the village schoolmaster, hinted one day to the owner of the house that he might find the Record Office interesting. Papers in the Record Office were duly searched and the *Inquisitiones post Mortem* for the Hundred disclosed a remarkable state of affairs. It appeared that from some time during the reign of James I there had been irregular periods of a year or so during which a shocking number of suicides had taken place in or on the edge of the quarry pond in the garden. These batches of suicides were separated from one another by irregular periods of up to fifty or sixty years during which nothing happened. There was no regularity in the length of any of the periods or in the number of suicides which took place in any group. It was noticed however that, for example, a farmer living seven or eight miles away, who had evidently decided to take his own life for certain reasons of his own which were disclosed at the inquest, had walked eight miles to the edge of the pond and shot himself there with a gun instead of doing so in his own farm. Others had hung themselves on trees near the pond, while others seem to have jumped into its waters.

Armed with these sinister facts and the full documentarian of recent happenings, the owner of the house, a Catholic, as had been said earlier, consulted the bishop of the diocese, who at first adopted an attitude of reserve until he had studied the dossier. Immediately thereafter he sent for the owner of the house and with the utmost gravity told him that he had decided on the evidence to use his episcopal powers and permit a full solemn exorcism of the house.

For those who have little knowledge of such matters, it may here be mentioned that permission for a solemn exorcism of this kind is very rarely granted: in fact, it is not easy to lay hands on the text or directions for the rite. The priest authorized by the bishop has to be specially selected or approved by him. Before performing the rite, which involves a Mass to be said anywhere in or near the haunted precincts, as the priest may choose, the latter is bound to observe an absolute fast for 24 hours beforehand, during which period he must be as far as possible in a state of prayer, in accordance with the statement of Our Lord that this kind goeth not out save by prayer and fasting. The episcopal authority allows the selected priest to perform the rite more than once for the same haunting in the event of the first exorcism apparently proving ineffective. This is in accordance with the Apostolic command to go on praying and not to faint. It also indicates the Church's recognition that we know little and are indeed not meant to know much in this world about the affairs of the next. It is not a question of science but of faith.

The main part of the exorcism consists, after special prayers, of a command in the name of Our Lord to the spirit to betake himself to the place appointed. The language used is terrific in its authority, unlike the usual quiet dignity of the Church's rites.

Before the exorcism could take place, a further experience was recorded. The witness knew about the previous phenomena, being a member of the small unofficial committee of inquiry, but, though a frequent visitor to the house, he had never previously experienced anything himself. For these reasons, he was personally inclined to disregard his own story as being of purely subjective origin. Ecclesiastical authority thought otherwise and directed that it should be included in the dossier.

This observer spent a night in the house over an Easter weekend. He occupied a bedroom in the newer portion, but one in which no phenomenon had been recorded as occurring up to that time. On the Saturday evening he went to bed shortly before midnight after a very cheerful party and, according to his own account, with no thought of the hauntings in his mind. He went to sleep but was woken some time during the night with the notion that somebody had called him by name. The impression was so strong that he got out of bed and opened the door into the passage, although the call was not repeated and the whole house seemed quiet. He did not turn on the lights since the room was nearly as bright as day with moonlight streaming in through the uncurtained windows. This witness observes that it was not until next morning that he remembered a connection between Easter and the full moon. After a moment or two looking up and down the passage he went back to bed, glancing at his watch as he did so. The time shown was exactly two minutes past three. This is of particular interest, since on using this argument to convince others that the affair was unconnected with the ghost, he found his argument turned against himself, since he had forgotten that Summer Time was in force, so that the true Greenwich Mean Time was two minutes past two and his awakening must have taken place almost exactly at 2 o'clock.

This witness's statement records that he lay down in bed and tried to turn over preparatory to going to sleep again when, to his great disquiet, he found himself paralysed. Not only was he unable to turn over but he could not move his head or his limbs, although he found he could open and shut his eyes. His first thought was that he must somehow have ricked his back or done himself some other physical damage. Before he could decide what to do, if anything, whether to call out for help or to wait and see if the apparent paralysis passed off, he became aware, without sight or sound, that something indescribable, a personality, but one utterly repugnant and hostile to himself, was arriving from a very great distance at a very great speed. The "thing" seemed to arrive and the witness confesses that he was frankly terrified. Invisible and inaudible though it remained, the thing seemed nevertheless in some way to dart at the witness, whereupon something else, of which the witness had in no way been conscious up to that time, seemed to intervene and throw the first thing off. The witness states that he prayed hard and went on doing so. Not once, but many times, the unpleasant thing hovering round seemed to make sudden darts at the witness, only to be repulsed each time by the intervention of the other thing. This very unpleasant experience went on until suddenly the witness heard a cock crow. The phenomenon ceased instantly. The witness, finding he could move, got up and looked at his watch. Three hours had elapsed; the sun was just rising, but he did not go to bed again although all sense of fear had left him, so that until called officially that morning, he slept peacefully in a chair, discovering that his mattress was wringing wet with the sweat that had poured from him during his dream or ordeal.

The exorcism was duly performed; the selected priest being one who had made a certain study of alleged occult happenings. He chose to say the Mass in the room wherein the child had complained of the "mice," giving as his reason, which he insisted must be taken as purely experimental, first that the child's experiences were possibly the earliest of the series, and secondly that the room itself might be, in picturesque terms, the "gateway of the monster," and the fact that any human had slept there might have provided the means of unlocking that gate. In view of the apparent connection between the strength of the manifestations and the Lunar cycle, the priest elected to say his Mass and perform the rite on a day on which the moon was full.

Nothing happened during the Mass or the rite, which naturally took place in the morning before breakfast. That night, however, two people sleeping in the house in rooms overlooking the lawn with the pond were woken by a noise which they likened to the howling of dogs, apparently coming from the lawn outside. The moon was full and the night was cloudless; whence it was apparent that there was nothing visible on the lawn which could be held responsible for the sounds, though the spot they were apparently coming from could be identified with certainty. The time was exactly two o'clock in the morning. As the watchers gazed in horror at the empty lawn, the sound of howling began to recede in jerks, as though something was being thrust farther and farther away. It faded into the distance and could no longer be heard. Since that date there has been no trouble in the house.

Made in the USA
Middletown, DE
05 September 2020

18379133R00118